G000241550

The Power of Personal

Jo — It's all about
P2P !..
Enjoy! Liz x

Liz Whitaker

R∃THINK PRESS

First published in Great Britain 2019
by Rethink Press (www.rethinkpress.com)

Illustrations from Propella® business intelligence software created by Ascend Studio

Propella® is a registered trademark owned by Condor Communications Limited

The design of the Propella grid in its entirety and parts are design rights registered with the Intellectual Property Office, design rights 6047140 to 6047176.

Cartoons by Tom Fishburne, Marketoonist

Cover design by Ascend Studio

I am very grateful to everyone who has contributed to *The Power of Personal* with interviews, case studies, and quotes. Please note these contributions do not indicate endorsement of the Propella software or process.

'This book hits a lot of the right spots for me: how to future proof client relationships, leverage internal talent and ensure that time and money spent on marketing are well spent. It's thought-provoking and accessible. Reading it has been a good investment of my time.'

— **David Fennell** Chief Executive, Gowling WLG

'Too many law firms, for far too long, have marketed by telling clients what the law firm is good at and can do, rather than by finding out what it is the client needs and wants the law firm to do. One of the book's central themes is about knowing a client's business as well as they know it themselves, and that must be the aspiration for all law firms looking to retain clients and win new business.'

— **Peter Rees QC** 39 Essex Chambers

'*The Power of Personal* debunks the theory that any communication is good communication and goes back to the time when personal interaction made a real difference.'

— **Grant Anthony** Partner at Crowe UK

'In our increasingly algorithmic artificial world, Liz explains why the power of personal communication is more – much more – important than ever. Business is rife with lazy communication. Be different, be more thoughtful. Steal a march on competitors. Read this book.'

— **Simon Slater** CEO

'If you want your marketing to stand out from the crowd and get you the results that you have always wanted, I highly recommend that you read *The Power of Personal* and really apply the lessons learned.'
  — **Derek Allen Mason** CEng PrEng MSc(Eng)
    MSAICE MICE MIStructE
    Founding Director of Super Structures
    Associates Limited

'My focus is on the numbers, so any book that shows us (with this degree of class) how to protect and grow the 20% that provides the 80% – which might then easily increase profits exponentially – is my perfect read!'
  — **Glyn Morris** Partner – Head of Finance (non-
    lawyer), Higgs & Sons

'Twenty-two years of talking to good clients about what they really value confirms strong relationships are top of the list. *The Power of Personal* gives a brilliant structure and approach that even those at the top of their game would find invaluable.'
  — **Nicola Duke** Head of Client Care,
    Mills & Reeve

'I'm all for finding technology that makes life easier and maximises value for the ultimate client. *The Power of Personal* combined with the Propella software hits that spot. It's clever and gives firms what they're looking for in their marketing. The advantage.'
  — **Derek Southall** CEO Hyperscale
    Group Limited

'Like many barristers I'm a reluctant marketeer. However, using the thinking outlined in this book was well within my comfort zone. Quite simply it showed me how to build a practice with people I already knew. No dramas, no difficult conversations, no extra work for the clerks.'
— **Jonathan Davies** Barrister,
Serjeants' Inn Chambers

'In our work to obtain new clients we used the thinking behind *The Power of Personal* to convert a random unstructured approach into a focused one. This helped us to identify the appropriate clients for our business and their relevant business needs. Success came quickly and some of our significant growth is down to this thinking.'
— **Nick O'Hara** Managing Director,
Thursfields Solicitors

'This is the book I have been waiting for. The "silver bullet" to developing a business pipeline is making mutual and meaningful connections. That's what you get here. It doesn't matter if you are new to marketing or already have an established career, *The Power of Personal* deserves a spot on your bookshelf.'
— **Maeve Jackson**
Marketing and BD Director

'The tried and tested PACE methodology and pipeline is all about showing professional firms how to win more of the right work from the right clients at the right price. Here is a book that makes clever use of communications to achieve exactly that at every stage of the PACE journey.'
— **John Monks** Managing Partner,
    The PACE Partners

'What stood out for me was the realisation that, despite the age of technology we live in, people still buy from people and we have all lost sight of that personal touch. The book brings this back to the forefront of our minds.'
— **Teresa Pugh** Practice Manager,
    New Park Court Chambers

To Kate GG, Beth, Ella, Miranda and
Clemmie for making all the difference

Contents

Foreword

by Susan Dunn,
Founder Harbour Litigation Funding

Time is our most precious commodity; we never have enough and we cannot buy more. The single biggest benefit of following this book's methodology is that it helps you spend your precious time more effectively.

This is how it worked for me.

In 2002, I set up my first litigation funding business with £1 million and an office in a former Kidderminster carpet factory. We were, and still are, pioneers in the litigation funding space. And therein was our first marketing challenge – how to create demand for an innovative, attractive service in a market famous for tradition and precedent.

Alongside that came the positioning of Harbour Litigation Funding as the pre-eminent brand with immediate access to significant funds and a peerless investment committee. And, importantly, the constant challenge to find good cases.

We put Harbour people at the forefront of the business to build relationships with the right people in law firms, chambers, insolvency practitioners, and corporates. We aimed high.

From the start we decided that people seeking funding would always speak to a real person, not fill in a form to reach an expert. We put clever, committed, and case-hungry people on the frontline.

Harbour Litigation Funding is now a global enterprise managing funds worth £760 million and claims in 15 major jurisdictions. In less than 20 years, litigation funding has become mainstream.

To achieve that growth and positioning we had to be selective.

As an entrepreneur I'm the type of person who gets excited about new opportunities, and I see the opportunity in everything. There simply aren't enough hours in the day to go after every opportunity, to build relationships with every lead. I needed to focus my time and energy, which is where Liz's grid and thinking came in.

By having the structure, tools, and discipline to focus on the people who will make a difference to your business, you stop chasing those who won't.

Our marketing was planned around achieving a specific and ambitious number of monthly case enquiries. Everyone in the team was focused on what Liz would call our 'mission'.

Yes, we had the usual marketing 'babble', the background noise. But the real results, the cases, came by building relationships with a relatively small number of people.

Using criteria specific to us, we identified our priority firms and chambers. We worked with our early adopters, the forward-thinking litigators, barristers, clerks, and others who could see how funding could transform a client's litigation chances. They became our internal ambassadors, an extension of the Harbour team.

Along the way we encountered the naysayers who preferred the status quo. Rather than dilute resources to convince them, we bestowed our full attention on those whose buy-in mattered and were open to dialogue.

Our messaging was always strong and backed by facts, figures, and case studies, which demonstrated the practical benefits of funding.

We thought about how to create bespoke dialogue and manage our interactions. Unlike some of the marketing I receive, I never assume that my interests are the same as those of the person I am talking to. By putting myself in their place, I am better able to find common ground and offer something that makes speaking to me worth their time.

Very early on in my career I learned to ask questions, to be curious. It's amazing what people will tell you with the right questioning and by spotting the leads they give you in conversation. The thing is, by finding out what will make them pay attention, what's going on in their world, and how funding can help, no encounter needs ever feel like a 'cold call'.

Working with Liz transformed the way I go about marketing without dampening my entrepreneurial spirit. It has become a way of life – part and parcel of the way I run my business. Using the power of the personal has channelled my energies into proactive and productive activities which have allowed Harbour to grow and succeed.

Now that Liz has distilled her thinking, approach, and advice into this book, you can benefit from her experience. Liz makes no bones about the fact that applying the power of personal is challenging.

I have been that person writing bespoke emails to key contacts with in-advance news about milestone developments like our new funds, case success, and high-profile appointments. I have hosted countless private dining events so we can find out more about what people are looking for in funding and unlock the relationship potential.

I have personally followed up so many interactions with thank-you letters, introductions, and connections. I have to tell you that it's also very enjoyable.

This is constant and ongoing. It's for the long term. As soon as one mission is achieved then another one begins.

Reading this book will lead you to think about people in a different way. You'll stop seeing them as a mass and start thinking about them as individuals. You'll prioritise those who can help you and you'll know how to make them pay attention and take the action you want.

I recommend you read it. It will work for any organisation. If you follow its simple steps, you will get results.
— Susan Dunn
Founder, Harbour Litigation Funding
www.harbourlitigationfunding.com

Introduction

More work. Top talent. An easier life. That's what any professional services leader and partner wants for their business and themselves.

But selling high-value professional services in a fiercely competitive market is monumentally hard work and, for some, relentlessly unrewarding. For most professionals, marketing, business development, sales, PR, communications, or whatever it comes dressed as (these terms are used interchangeably) is *not* what you came into your profession to do.

I'm about to show you that the solution is staring you in the face. It's on the tip of your tongue and in your hands. Literally. It's already there in your client database, networks, and payroll. You might *think* you're working in a business-to-business (B2B) or business-to-consumer (B2C) business. You're not. You're in the person-to-person (P2P) business.

The Power of Personal will show you how to find the diamonds in all that data. By connecting, convincing, and creating exceptional client relationships, you will build a competitive advantage that perfectly positions you to win more work and keep and recruit top talent.

To quote one very satisfied lawyer using this approach: 'You can stuff the competition.' *The Power of Personal* gives you a P2P marketing toolkit to win hearts and minds, shift opinion, and secure loyalty levels you thought belonged in the past.

Who are you?

Before you set out on the Propella journey, there are some prequalification criteria.

The Power of Personal works for organisations selling high-value services in highly competitive markets. You will know the names of the people who matter, or it's easy to find them. Law firms, chambers, accountants, membership associations, independent schools, financial services, private wealth management, construction/property professionals, consultants, investor relations, charities/third sector, medical/

aesthetic services, design and creative businesses, and entrepreneurs can all benefit from this approach. Readers from these sectors, please swap the professional services vocabulary for your own.

The common denominator is that for your clients, there is a financial or reputational risk involved in choosing you. Trust is paramount, so it's crucial to create and *maintain* a relationship with your clients.

Extrovert or introvert, the Propella methodology can work for you. But what distinguishes my most successful clients is this: ambition.

You are on a mission to achieve something, and success is important for career, financial, or life reasons. You're smart and on top of your game. Your work really *matters* to you – it's not just a job. Oh, and you might be a teeny-weeny bit competitive.

Driven, yes. Very. Your full-time work is doing what you qualified to do, but you have a 'marketing/business growth responsibility' which needs to fit around the work. You and other fee earners have very limited or zero time or money for marketing. It certainly needs to be justified. Marketing skills and know-how might also be in short supply. You may or may not have marketing professionals advising you. You have a track record of satisfied clients and contacts. You rely on your team to deliver the organisation's advice, services, and total experience.

It's hard to get your voice heard out there, hard to get the edge, especially if you're a new, disruptor, or challenger brand competing with established (aka safe) players. Or you could be that established brand and need to update old perceptions.

You have to pitch for work and your reward may depend on what you bring in. You may have a management board and/or shareholders to keep happy. Your success is visible and possibly monitored by others. If you're not accountable to someone else, you're accountable to yourself.

You are also authentic, the real deal. You'll need that because *The Power of Personal* requires you to give something of yourself.

You might also be a current or aspirational CEO, practice manager, senior clerk, or marketing professional advising the above.

Truly ambitious people always reach their goals. Using the Propella methodology will speed things up.

My story

I've worked in and around professional services marketing for over thirty years. That's included in-house and consultancy roles advising big, small, international, national, regional, and boutique firms, as well as membership associations, while working with partners, barristers, chief executives, practice managers, clerks, owners, and people *aspiring* to be one of these. They all want the same outcome: growth from existing and new clients, stability from people retention, and smooth recruitment of top talent. No matter what the client's size, type, or location, when I go behind the business façade, I will find one or more of at least 100 mistakes they are making which limit the potential of its marketing communications to achieve those successful outcomes.

I created the Propella process to avoid all these mistakes. Underpinning the process is the absolute truth that people buy from people, and they always will. That's what this book is about.

People also *work* for people, *vote* for people, *support* people, *donate* to people, *move mountains* for people. Future Propella grids will be created to support HR and organisations focused on voters, supporters, and donations.

Propella works. I've used it countless times. It's been eye-opening, game-changing, and often a relief for those using it.

Propella's origins go back to my parents' shop, where my teenage self worked on Saturdays and during holidays. In this business, respecting discretionary spend and looking after customers meant these customers came back. That meant more sales (although then, to be honest, my motivation was saving for David Cassidy LPs).

Later, armed with an English degree and an attitude, I started my career with Central Independent Television, a listed independent television company, which taught me a) the value of planning ahead for financial and reputational success and b) how marketing and communications could have a whopping strategic purpose and financial benefit.[1] It wasn't for decoration.

From there, it was into professional services. During my time as Director of Corporate Communications for what was then Wragge & Co, I was introduced to the stakeholder grid. That was the spark that ignited what is now Propella.

---

1   In the 1991 franchise auction, Central Independent Television retained its franchise with a bid of £2,000 per year (fundinguniverse.com). To put this in context, Thames Television bid £33 million for its franchise and lost to Carlton Television, which bid £42 million (screenonline.org.uk)

In your hands you have a large dose of hindsight: the lessons I've learned so you don't have to. There are also observations borrowed from other sectors. Much of my client work referenced is confidential, but all the stories are true.

Of the quotations used, the quintessential one is 'Only connect...', from E. M. Forster's *Howards End*.[2] Firms are full of people eager to do good things but who have become disconnected from those who would be happy to help them – if only they could connect. By the end of this book, you will know how to identify and *meaningfully* connect with exactly these people.

How to use this book

This book takes you on the Propella journey, from Prepare then to Plot, Prioritise, Plan, Personalise, Perfect, and Prepare (again).

Propella philosophy sits at the unexplored intersection between personalisation and technology. It's the best of the past, present, and future. This is smart thinking, and I recommend reading the book in the context of *your* goals.

---

2   E. M. Forster, *Howards End* (London: Edward Arnold, 1910)

Professionals enjoy an explanation, so we start with why and consider what's happening in the world and to us. In the Prepare section, we lay the groundwork for creating the best possible circumstances to connect, convince, and create exceptional client relationships. You'll see how to avoid facelessness and improve your appreciation of people managing your invisible and visible touchpoints. I also share some tips that could mean the difference between communications success and failure.

Then we move into Plot, Prioritise, and Plan. This is where the magic starts to happen. You will be introduced to the Propella methodology, so you can plot the *priority* groups, organisations, and people who will make *your* success a reality. Professionals love Propella logic. You'll meet ten characters, starting with the most highly prized, the Ambassador, and learn what to do with them. This is all original material created by me based on years of business and people watching.

We finish with two chapters on personalised communication: Think Big, followed by Act Small. Perfect is about delivering the best possible marketing communications, and the final Prepare is about preparing for the success it brings. Don't complain to me if your diary is full of invitations, conversations, and more work!

I recommend reading this book from start to finish. Then, once you've 'got' how Propella works, you can dip in again wherever you wish. The Propella process can bring clarity to various situations, including merger-candidate search, event management, and crisis navigation. The Propella business intelligence software is a live, real-time, and shareable tool, but please be reassured that you don't *need* the software to apply the Propella principles or any of the advice shared in this book.

Finally...

More work and top talent I can guarantee – if you follow the process.

An easier life? Ha, that might be trickier. But I can promise that time spent on marketing will deliver a result.

Think fulfilment not frustration. Think enjoyment not exhaustion. There will be magic, rather than manic, marketing moments of connecting, convincing, and creating exceptional client relationships.

The easy bit is realising you can just be yourself.

SECTION 1
THE BIG FAT WHY?

*(Although I've yet to meet anyone
who thinks this is a bad idea.)*

CHAPTER ONE

What's Happening In The World

This chapter is about what's happening in the world that makes *The Power of Personal* matter now.

The next is about what's happening to us.

My bet is you will quietly nod your head and underline, or be reassured by, at least one of the following fifteen influences, ideas, and 'nowisms' (because you've thought this yourself). I'm sharing them now because you may need to revisit them when a) you're writing personal messages on top of everything else, and b) you need to convince colleagues.

One/15 – Relationship capital – a new currency

Not on your radar? It will be. Broadly defined, 're-lationship capital' is the value of relationships with people essential to your business success. In *The Power of Personal*, we call them 'stakeholders'.

Relationship capital doesn't (yet) appear on a bal-ance sheet, but you know instinctively that it matters. Seemingly intangible and mostly taken for granted, it's invisible until threatened. Think of it as currency, equal in importance to the bottom line.

Stakeholder reputation is a net contributor to rela-tionship capital. And that can be lost in a moment (the 'Gerald Ratner prawn sandwich'[3] is still a jaw-dropping example). It cannot be delegated or ignored. Now is the time to invest in those hard-earned rela-tionships. As this book will reveal, they represent a wealth of often untapped potential to achieve goals and are invaluable if reputation is threatened.

---

3   In the 1980s, Gerald Ratner built a profitable jewellery empire, Ratners. In a famous keynote address to the Institute of Directors, he referred to one product as 'total crap' and to one set of earrings as 'cheaper than an M&S prawn sandwich but probably wouldn't last as long'. The value of Ratners fell by £500 million almost overnight, profits turned into a £122.3 million loss, and 330 shops closed. To make such a gaffe is sometimes called 'doing a Ratner'. www.thisismoney.co.uk/money/markets/article-2371730/GERALD-RATNER-INTERVIEW-How-I-cut-cr-p--The-return-UKs-biggest-online-jeweller.html

My go-to source for all things reputational is Leslie Gaines-Ross, author and chief reputation strategist at Weber Shandwick in NYC. Although her work is focused on corporate America, everything translates to professional firm leadership. In her game-changing book *CEO Capital – A Guide to Building CEO Reputation and Company Success*, Gaines-Ross includes extensive research that proves the link between reputation management (especially around the CEO) and an organisation's financial success.[4]

In a personal interview for this book, she said:

> 'Relationship capital is more critical than ever because it is harder to grasp due to everything being diluted by online relationship building. Such rarity means we recognise it when we see it or feel it but especially when it is absent. It's tangible, not transactional. Here is this asset with the potential to create lasting competitive advantage. Relationship capital doesn't just happen – it needs to be earned, managed and protected until it's the very foundation of good business. And it starts at the top with leaders who set the standard by putting their people first, communicating openly and honestly, respecting the client's spend and choice.'

---

4   L. Gaines-Ross, *CEO Capital: A Guide to Building CEO Reputation and Company Success* (Hoboken, NJ: John Wiley & Sons, 2003).

The Propella methodology is a tool to manage, appreciate, and protect your relationship capital.

Two/15 – Marketing is one big noise

Here's how it is for most of us. Inbox overload. Spam. Social media bombardment. Intrusive, inappropriate advertising based on our Google searches. Nuisance sales calls. Chuggers. Rubbish through our letterbox. Newspapers and magazines full of leaflets, flyers, and other printed nonsense using up precious resources. Shouty people between the music on the radio. Constant noise in our faces.

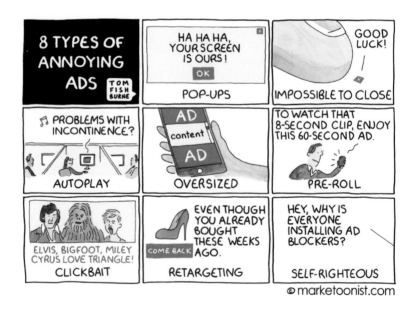

© marketoonist.com

It's not smart, it's not clever, and it's not working. The famous John Wanamaker quote still applies to much marketing: 'Half the money I spend on advertising is wasted; the trouble is I don't know which half.'

Global customer experience expert Larry Hochman, in his book *The Relationship Revolution: Closing the Customer Promise Gap*, states that 'the revolutionary battle with your customers in the future is likely to be a battle for their attentions'.[5]

Most of what passes as 'marketing', 'communications', or 'PR' is background noise (aka blah). It's just 'there', and regardless of the source it all sounds the same. Even the interesting stuff is lost in the blah, and increasingly, we're not sure if it's authentic or fake blah.

In *Zag: The #1 Strategy of High-Performance Brands*, Marty Neumeier calls this 'clutter' – product clutter, feature clutter, advertising clutter, message clutter, and media clutter.[6]

The Power of Personal explains how to cut through that clutter.

---

5   L. Hochman, *The Relationship Revolution: Closing the Customer Promise Gap* (Hoboken, NJ: John Wiley & Sons, 2010).
6   M. Neumeier, *Zag: The #1 Strategy of High-Performance Brands* (Berkeley, CA: New Riders, 2007).

Three/15 – Commoditised marketing is dehumanising

By commoditised marketing, I mean the wholesale distribution of 'noise' through the database, including:

- Newsletters with content that's 90% irrelevant to most readers

- The 'Dear Client' email

- A leaflet/brochure minus a compliment slip

- A press conference for all media

- Mass invitations to crowded events where no one in charge appears to know or care if you came

At best, it keeps people informed; at worst, irritated and feeling unimportant.

Commoditised marketing makes a lot of noise in an echo chamber. Despite the work and expense of pushing it out, it meets the needs of none of the people, none of the time. It's a mistake for organisations selling high-value services to rely solely on this for marketing.

Because it's easy and cheap, technology has fuelled commoditised marketing. But easy and cheap does not equal effective. Commoditised marketing doesn't work because people are not commodities. People buying high-value services want reassurance that, *at the very least*, you know their name, especially in an existing relationship.

Referring to the explosion of new technologies in Silicon Valley, social business strategist and instigator of the #H2H (Human to Human) business movement, Bryan Kramer said:

> 'We needed to bring back the human side of communication, in all its imperfection, empathy and simplicity. I sense that others have hit the same threshold in craving the real and authentic side of us all. That is what inspired H2H.'[7]

Commoditised communication is acceptable in crisis situations where an urgent message must immediately reach a large number of people.

Four/15 – The new power in word of mouth

Hands up if you've booked a hotel room, chosen a restaurant, ordered running shoes or a new waste bin on the recommendation of a complete stranger.

---

7   B. Kramer, *There is No B2B or B2C: It's Human to Human*, H2H (Bryan Kramer, 2014).

My hand is up. And that's just today.

Larry Hochman says, 'Word of mouth and reputation are now far, far more important than advertising. The terrifying and exciting thing is that, unlike advertising, you can't buy word of mouth.'[8]

Malcolm Gladwell flagged up its value in *The Tipping Point: How Little Things Can Make a Big Difference*: 'Because of the sheer ubiquity of marketing efforts these days, word of mouth appeals have become the only kind of persuasion that most of us respond to anymore.'[9]

When exploring what he calls 'agents of change' driving word of mouth, he says, 'The success of any kind of social epidemic is heavily dependent on the involvement of people with a particular and rare set of social gifts.'

He identifies three types of people – Connectors, Mavens, and Salesmen. You'll know these people.

Connectors are well-networked people who know how to bring the right people together and make connections. Mavens are those with lots of knowledge; the go-to, reliable people on particular issues. Salesmen

---

8   Hochman, *The Relationship Revolution*.
9   M. Gladwell, *The Tipping Point: How Little Things Can Make a Big Difference* (New York: Little, Brown and Company, 2000).

are self-explanatory; they have the gifts of charisma and persuasion.

My theory is that all three are often found in the same person.

The Power of Personal will show you how to a) identify Gladwell's Connectors, Mavens, and Salesmen in your client database, in your phone, and on your payroll and b) how to manage word of mouth.

Five/15 – Find your innovators and adopters

Everett Rogers' Diffusion of Innovations theory[10] is enjoying a renaissance thanks to Simon Sinek's TED talk 'How great leaders inspire action'[11] and Geoffrey A. Moore's book *Crossing the Chasm*.[12]

Quick definition.

Innovators take risks for an idea, product, or service, even without a following. These visionaries, first in

---

10 E. Rogers, *Diffusion of Innovations* (New York, NY: The Free Press, a Division of Simon & Schuster, Inc., 1962).

11 Simon Sinek, 'How great leaders inspire action' [video], TEDxPuget Sound, September 2009. https://www.ted.com/talks/simon_sinek_how_great_leaders_inspire_action.

12 G. A. Moore, *Crossing the Chasm* (New York, NY: Harper Business Essentials, 1991).

line for anything new, are your go-to-first 'marketing' department.

Close behind are the **early adopters**, the trendsetters or opinion formers. Possibly influenced by the innovators, they've filtered the choices and like to be seen as first to try new things. **Late adopters** come next.

Then you know the routine. Early majority, late majority, and, finally laggards.

Think about which of your clients, contacts, and employees are innovators and early adopters. Capture those names because you'll need them later.

Six/15 – Times have changed

Larry Hochman best sums it up:

> 'Tough times have changed what [customers]
> value, who they trust, how and what they wish
> to purchase… Let down, exhausted, feeling
> out of control, they are seeking the stability
> of business relationships where companies
> feel loyal to them, where small kindnesses are
> practised, where recognition is commonplace,

where simplicity and speed are the rule, not the exception.'[13]

In a competitive market, buyers with discretionary spend *and* choice expect more. And they want it fast. They want a *relationship*, something for the long term in an uncertain world. People seek organisations that reflect *their* values. People buying high-value services in a competitive market enjoy the luxury of control over where they spend their money.

Hochman makes a valid point:

> 'Almost everything in your business can be replicated. Competing on price and product is easy. The only things that can't be replicated are the relationships you have with your customers. The one-to-one interactions that you build up with them, over days, weeks, months and years are truly unique and truly earned.'[14]

The Power of Personal shows you how to deliver loyalty and recognition in your marketing communications.

---

13 Hochman, *The Relationship Revolution*.
14 Hochman, *The Relationship Revolution*.

Seven/15 – It's all about 'customer experience' now

Some industry sectors have added Customer Experience Directors to their marketing teams.

A McKinsey CEO guide to customer experience concludes: 'Companies that create exceptional customer experiences can set themselves apart from their competitors.' The guide highlights how customer experience leaders can 'build customer loyalty, make employees happier, achieve revenue gains of 5 to 10 percent and reduce costs by 15 to 25 percent within two or three years'.[15]

The new kid on the job-title block is Director of/ Manager of/Head of Customer Success. This is the direction of travel.

Imagine the service expectations of clients or targets with these in-house people.

---

15 McKinsey&Company, 'The CEO guide to customer experience', *McKinsey Quarterly* (August 2016), Executive Briefing. https://www.mckinsey.com/business-functions/operations/our-insights/the-ceo-guide-to-customer-experience.

Eight/15 – Artificial intelligence will never replace...

… charisma, charm, kindness, and caring.

It will never replace the joy of connection sparked by P2P.

Standout, memorable, and successful organisations will always have people at the forefront.

Think about how you make decisions to buy, support, recommend, vote, or donate. A connection with a person makes these decisions a more meaningful experience. Even routine purchases are so much more enjoyable when the person serving your coffee, hanging up your coat, or delivering your groceries is authentic and a bit smiley.

In your travels today, assess the connections you make with people you meet, those representing their employers, and ask yourself how they leave you *feeling*.

That's what's happening in the world.

Now, a look at what's happening to us. Or not happening.

CHAPTER TWO

What's Happening To Us

What's happening to us, or not happening, that makes *The Power of Personal* matter now is covered in this chapter.

Nine/15 – Individual differences

Generations

Many organisations face the challenge of communicating with different generations *at the same time*. But the style, emphasis, and delivery of Baby Boomer marketing communications could alienate, not appeal to, a Millennial. And vice versa.

It's natural to want to communicate with people using our own generational style. In professional firms, Baby Boomers and Generation X tend to have authority and wealth, while clients and employees are increasingly Generation Y (aka Millennials) and Generation Z. So there is immediate disparity.

People of all generations, for different reasons, want to be treated as individuals.

In a contribution for this book, Moira Clark, Professor of Strategic Marketing at Henley Business School[16], provided the following definitions of generation groups in the UK (italics are mine, to emphasise why personalisation is important for each group).

Baby Boomers (born 1945–1965) are shaped by the economic boom, man on the moon, and the 1966 World Cup. The workaholic Baby Boomers are team focused, like to be in control, are image conscious, and nostalgic. In their heads, they are forever forty! They hold 75% of the UK's wealth and are responsible for 50% of all consumer spending. *They appreciate and pay extra for additional service.*

Generation X (born 1965–1989) are shaped by the Winter of Discontent, IRA bombings, and the fall of communism. They are not scared of failure, and *value experiences and relationships.* They are concept loyal,

---

16 https://www.henley.ac.uk/people/person/professor-moira-clark.

not brand loyal. Immediate gratification is important to them. They like self-service customer support and shopping online.

Generation Y (born from 1990) are optimistic, confident, and globally aware. They are serious multi-taskers and think nothing of consuming multiple media on multiple devices. They are tech savvy, so brands must facilitate engagement through technology if they want to target this group, *through building relationships* and providing them with a comprehensive self-service option for support. For this group, customer-to-customer interaction is more important than business-to-consumer.

If you have clients, contacts, or employees from the **Silent Generation** (born 1925–1944), you don't need me to tell you that these people appreciate being treated more formally and as individuals, for a whole variety of reasons. Those of us lucky enough to still have living family members from this generation also appreciate it on their behalf.

Cultures and countries

Most organisations have global clients, targets, influencers, employees, potential employees, and suppliers. English might be the universal business language, but it's easily misinterpreted. Cultural differences add a complexity that means one-size-fits-all marketing communications do *not* work, and might even be damaging. Think about the potential for misunderstanding around salutation, vocabulary, body language, dress codes, and etiquette.

Left- and right-brainers

Left-brain dominant people are strong on logic, analytics, language, reasoning, science, and numbers; while right-brain dominant people excel in creativity, the arts, imagination, intuition, insight, and holistic thoughts. It's obvious that a sales-based communication to an accountancy or legal practice would need a different emphasis than one directed to an entrepreneur-led business. Personalising the communication for different groups, if not individuals, increases its impact.

Males and females

In my experience, males and females communicate differently from each other and respond to different triggers. Again, one size does not fit all, so securing some middle ground is ideal. Problems arise from thoughtless, avoidable extremes:

- The accountancy firm whose annual corporate hospitality event is held at a rugby match in the boozy box (clearly aimed at men and holds zero appeal for many female clients or people from alcohol-abstinent cultures); worse still is the 'make-up and Prosecco' event for the female clients!

- The assumption that a business director must be male as evident in the automated 'Dear Sir'

- The pitch team of over-forty-five white males to a target led by a young female director

- The website where men are clearly in charge and women are secretaries

Does it matter? Yes, it does.

Using *The Power of Personal* means you can reflect and respect the different people types in your clients, targets, and employees.

Ten/15 – Humans are animals

Notwithstanding that in the First World we live in sophisticated times, as outlined above, humans are still, fundamentally, animals.

We function in hierarchies, either social or created (such as the British class and Indian caste systems). Our individual survival depends on trust in others, and instinct determines that trust. We must *trust* the people who want our money, our opinions, our support, our votes or to change our behaviour.

But it's more than trust. We want to know the following: *Is this person in the right position in the hierarchy? Is this person acknowledging where I am in the hierarchy? Is this person in my tribe? Is this person friend or foe?*

We make instant gut decisions by looking into a person's face, particularly their eyes, and reading their gestures, body language, clothes, accessories, and even their health.

Are they dressed to impress or insult us? Are they groomed in a way that shows effort and respect? We listen to their voice, more *how* they say something than what they say. We observe their manner. What do they give of themselves to symbolise the importance of the relationship? We 'feel' authenticity. A zillion movements are calculated in a nanosecond. This can never, ever, be faked.

'Authenticity has repeatedly proved to be a key differentiator of performance in winning work', said executive coach Cathy Walton, in an exclusive interview for this book. Walton has over twenty-five years' experience working with partners to improve their business development skills.[17]

---

17 Cathy Walton can be contacted via LinkedIn.

'Authenticity means having more meaningful relationships because when you are genuine, people know it. Everyone can spot a faker, even if they can't articulate why. Whether it's the critical factor in a pitch team winning a new key account or a partner in a law firm establishing their status as a trusted adviser, competence is assumed; reliability and credibility is expected, but building a personal connection is what makes the difference. The trick is always to identify where the real you overlaps with the needs of the audience such that there is a fit. This results in a connection that is real and is felt.'

How are any of us supposed to make a trust-based decision on a one-size-fits-all communication that gives absolutely nothing of the person who sent it? It speaks, without saying a word, 'You don't matter.'

That's why people buy from people. They always have and they always will.

Eleven/15 – Tribes matter to humans

Humans want to belong to tribes. Brands are the new tribes. People heading up firms are the contemporary equivalents of tribal leaders. The senior team members are tribal elders. Employees represent the tribe.

When purchasing or recommending high-value services, buyers choose their tribe by looking for themselves and where they will be most welcome. Belonging to the tribe represents a place of safety, of being connected, of pride.

The right communications secure loyalty to your tribe.

Twelve/15 – Google's Zero Moment of Truth – 7 hours, 11 touches, 4 locations

Everyone and anyone interacting with your business is on a journey. There is a starting point, and then, for some, an engagement point, which could be buying a service, introducing a contact, or becoming an employee. If you get it right, the journey continues into further engagement territory. These journeys could take days, weeks, months, or years. Along those journeys, people will make decisions about your organisation by interacting with various touchpoints. A bad experience at any touchpoint could cause them to turn away.

In the olden days, that is BG (Before Google), you sort of 'knew' that potential clients and contacts were moving in your direction on that journey. A few lunches, a bit of networking, your own events, exploratory meetings, informal chats, the seeking of references – eventually, that magic engagement moment would come.

It's all a bit more sophisticated now, and in highly competitive markets, a lot needs to be right for the journey to keep flowing.

Google's Zero Moment of Truth (ZMOT)[18] is the research journey taken by a potential buyer of consumer services making a decision. Google concluded that a buyer needs around 7 hours of interaction with an organisation across 11 touchpoints in 4 locations before making a commitment.

People buying high-value services are likely to take a similar buying journey even if they already know you. From the initial prompt, your potential buyer will look online (including from mobile devices) to gather information. Unless your buyer has 100% loyalty to you and/or you have no competitors, they will keep their options open.

Think about those 11 touchpoints. A touchpoint might be a brochure downloaded from your website, a LinkedIn update, attending an event, or asking someone about their experience of your organisation. They might even phone you.

Introducing personalisation into the ZMOT journey would vastly enrich the quality of that individual

---

18   Google, 'Zero Moment of Truth (ZMOT)', *Think with Google*. https://www.thinkwithgoogle.com/marketing-resources/micro-moments/zero-moment-truth/.

experience and may speed up, or even determine, the final decision in your favour. Who doesn't want to be top of the pitch pecking order? Better still, who would rather not have to pitch?

People 'touch' your organisation for a reason. Personalisation helps you to understand that reason, collect intelligence, and follow up effectively.

Throughout *The Power of Personal* we'll talk a lot about the stakeholder journey and how to manage it.

Thirteen/15 – Personal brand and personal network

You don't have a choice about having a personal reputation, but you *do* have a choice about how to manage it. Your personal brand determines where you are in the hierarchy, so be clear on where you *want* to be in the hierarchy. The people you choose to align yourself with significantly influences your personal brand.

Having thousands of contacts, friends, and followers is an asset, but the Propella methodology helps you to establish a circle of trust and manage that asset. Your *real* personal network is a reliable, manageable selection of people who accelerate your success.

On the other side of this, be very aware of whose personal network you choose to be in.

Fourteen/15 – The value of empathy

According to author Daniel Pink, in *A Whole New Mind – Why Right-Brainers Will Rule The Future*, we are moving from the Information Age to the Conceptual Age: 'Because of Abundance, businesses are realizing that the only way to differentiate their goods and services in today's overstocked marketplace is to make their offerings physically beautiful and emotionally compelling.' He says that to prepare for this new world, we must adopt six essential aptitudes. One is empathy, which he defines as 'the ability to imagine yourself in someone else's position and to intuit what that person is feeling. It is the ability to stand in others' shoes, to see with their eyes'.[19]

Empathy is everything in *The Power of Personal*.

---

19   D. H. Pink, *A Whole New Mind – Why Right-Brainers Will Rule The Future* (Singapore: Marshall Cavendish, 2008).

Fifteen/15 – Six degrees of separation is now two

BG there was the view that the world was so small, we were all only six degrees separated from each other. My belief is that social networks and our connected world now mean that we (certainly many readers of this book) are sometimes only two degrees separated from even the world's most powerful people.

Much easier to reach than the most powerful people are the potential clients and contacts who are already connected to people you know.

Why would you want to waste your time and resources pushing stuff out to anonymous people when, with some forethought and bravery, you can simply ask someone for an introduction?

Now you know why personalisation matters so much.

Next, we'll look at preparing to put personalisation back into your marketing.

SECTION 2
PREPARE

(The promised hindsight; the lessons I've learned so you don't have to.)

CHAPTER THREE

People And Touchpoints

In this chapter, we look at the people on both sides of P2P and explore the range of touchpoints used to form an opinion about your organisation.

Managing your touchpoints can enhance cross-selling, general sales, recruitment, and reputation management. This is how you gain 'the edge'.

Avoid facelessness

We start with the first P in P2P: you – the leader/ head/owner (I'll call you the Chief Ambassador) – and your senior team. You should be visible, accountable, and accessible and here's why. High-value services are bought from real people, not brands. A faceless organisation – that is, an organisation where the spotlight is on the brand, product, or service and people are absent from the communications – is instantly disadvantaged in the P2P world.

Faceless organisations arise for various reasons: technology makes it easy for people to hide behind brands; some introverted leaders prefer to stay out of the limelight (sorry, not an option, but the limelight can be made more comfortable); and internal politics can mean that popular and charismatic individuals are forbidden to front a brand (that said, there's a fine line between allowing magnetic personalities to shine and encouraging a dangerous cult of personality).

Dent Global, world leaders in entrepreneurial strategy, published a report[20] to help organisations explore strategies for safely developing personality brands within a corporate culture. The report states: 'It's nearly impossible for a faceless company to compete with a rival who has admired personalities standing side by side with their company brand.'

It points out that 'high achievers around the world want to align with great companies, great products and big vision, but they connect with these attributes through the people who are at the forefront'. Readers of *The Power of Personal* will almost certainly be targeting high achievers.

---

20   Dent Global, *Build An Influential Organisation*, www.dent.global/publications/

Dent's report concludes: 'In the realms of social media, the trend is clear – people trust faces a lot more than they trust logos.'

People will often choose a high-value service based on the perceived strength, capability, likeability, and personality of the Chief Ambassador, that is, the senior partner, Practice Manager, Chief Clerk, Managing Director, CEO (whatever title works in your organisation). They will also look at the board, the management committee, and the senior teams, even if they have never met you or any of these people. This is how to give the right impression from the start:

- Be visible, accessible, and accountable in primary communications.

- Take everything that technology offers, starting with video and social media, to bring you to life and to demonstrate what you stand for.

- Use professional, well-chosen photographs. People make subconscious choices based on images (do these professionals look successful, positive, approachable?).

- Ensure your profile is up to date, succinct, relevant, and conveys something of your personality.

- Be seen and heard for the right reasons. How are you promoting your firm's values?

- Be authentic, even when dealing with bad news.

Maximise face-to-face (F2F) contact with selected stakeholders. Your surprise presence at a pivotal moment can be a game changer. It says, 'You matter to us.' Even brief contact – a greeting, a handshake, and a few words of welcome – is enough to transform a simple event into an F2F personalised experience for the other person.

Beyond the leadership team – visible and invisible internal stakeholders

Q1. How many people are in the business?

Q2. How many people are in the marketing department?

The answer to the second question is the same as the answer to the first.

Think about *everyone* in the business as members of the marketing, PR, and recruitment departments. This is the tribe.

P2P is more than the leadership team and frontline professionals. It's impossible for them to be physically present at all touchpoints all the time, so everyone in the organisation must represent them at all times. Everyone must look successful, positive, and approachable. Everyone must understand the business, its goals, and its values and be motivated to contribute to its success. Buying decisions in professional services are also shaped by personal interactions with the following:

- Security

- Reception

- Switchboard

- Secretaries/personal assistants/virtual assistants

- The marketing team (event manager and website manager especially)

- Catering

- Clerks

- Practice managers

- Account managers

- Whoever answers the phone!

When I ask my clients which brands they admire the most, the following names make regular appearances: John Lewis/ Waitrose, Apple (the Genius Bars), Westmorland Motorway Services (better known as Tebay and Gloucester Services), Nespresso, First Direct, and Chiltern Railways. These are very different businesses that have the following in common: brilliant products and/or services, excellent customer experience at many touchpoints, corporate social responsibility, success, and, where relevant (and this is the best bit), price is not an issue. Without exception, they are standout and memorable because of their frontline people. Two are challenger brands in sectors with woefully low consumer popularity. Two are challenger brands in well-established sectors. One is the world's largest information technology company. One is a public transport company in a sector dogged by poor reputation and service levels. None have been afraid to invest in their people on the frontlines.

Then there are the invisible employees, who, often unknowingly, represent your organisation by managing vital touchpoints. Think about cleaners, security, backroom catering, and delivery people, including outsourced roles. If you've experienced a miserable cloakroom attendant or an intimidating security guard, you'll understand. The C-suite at United Airlines will always wish they'd thought about that.[21]

In my experience, it's often these invisible people who have the best ideas on how to improve processes that involve them. They also have influence with friends, family, neighbours, and a social media network. Like everyone else, they respond positively to being included and respected.

Include them in your communications. Say hello. Show interest in their work and lives. Thank them

---

21 To accommodate United Airlines staff on an overbooked flight, sixty-nine-year-old passenger David Dao was forced out of his seat and dragged down the aisle by Chicago Department of Aviation security officers. The incident was recorded by other passengers and shared on social and international media outlets.

for good work. They will remember how your words made them *feel* for a long, long time. Look at the world from their point of view.

Treat people with respect at this level and they are more likely to recommend your organisation as a great employer. They are more likely to take pride in their work, do a great job for you, go the extra mile, make discretionary effort, and think and act outside the nine to five. They are also more likely to defend you in a crisis.

Watch any episode of *Undercover Boss*[22] and you'll see my point.

Visible and invisible touchpoints

All day, every day, people are looking at your business for a reason. These people could be anywhere in the world or around the corner. Some you know, some you don't. Some you want, some you don't. They will 'touch' your business at one or more of several touchpoints. They are on their own journeys to engage, or not, with your organisation.

---

22 *Undercover Boss* is a reality television series. Each episode depicts a senior manager at a major business going undercover as an entry-level employee at their own organisation to discover the faults in the company.

Managing your touchpoints allows you to deliver the best possible experience. Some touchpoints are visible, some are invisible. Some may surprise you.

In Chapter 2, we referenced Google's ZMOT research – it takes a person 7 hours across 11 touchpoints in 4 locations to reach that elusive zero moment of truth: a decision, a commitment. My view is that personalisation at these touchpoints could triple their value and accelerate that journey.

When they're on this journey, people may be drawing comparisons between you and your competitors. They may drop you out of their journey if they don't like what they find or if your response is too slow. During that journey, they will rank you on a shortlist and eventually decide about their future relationship with you. Will they buy from you? Will they recommend you?

Also along this journey, people will be looking for themselves in your marketing and communications. Remember, we all want to be treated as individuals but we also want to find our tribe. We want to be reassured that we're in safe territory, that we're 'known' even though we've never met.

At Propella HQ, we've identified 100 generic visible and invisible touchpoints relevant to external and internal stakeholders. Others will be unique to your business.

They are all your responsibility.

Some scenarios

To get you into the mindset, here are some examples of standard stakeholder touchpoint journeys. These are much broader than website-user journeys, as you will see.

Existing buyers/clients/customers are in a **meeting room** working on a project. Before they arrived, they checked the website **people profiles** to see who they were meeting and spoke to your **secretary** about **parking**. On their way in, they came through **security** and **reception** and used **the loo**. Lunch is included (provided by outside **caterers**). Later, they want a **tour** of your building.

Prospective buyers/clients/customers conduct a **Google** search of your organisation and find words and **images**. They're scanning your **media coverage** before examining your sector expertise and team on your **website** to assess if a) the team knows what they're doing b) they like the look of them from their **photographs**. They're also asking around their **peer group** to find out who has experience working with you. Before the day is out, they **call your office** to ask for an appointment. The phone is unattended, so they listen to the **voicemail message**.

Satisfied client on project completion is taking your team out for a **celebration** with **other advisers**. Satisfied client would like to give you some **feedback** and reference your firm in their **media coverage**. Satisfied client is well connected on **LinkedIn**. The lead partner is about to email the **final invoice**, including a **time sheet**. Satisfied client will soon have a **requirement for further work** from other teams in your firm not yet used (although the existing suppliers are aware of this and have doubled their efforts to keep their client). Lead **partner** does not have an exemplary track record in cross-selling other services. Satisfied client is already thinking about how they can **keep in touch** with your firm.

A new and junior *journalist* who writes for a leading magazine is looking at a **report** you issued on **LinkedIn**. They're scanning your **website** and, under a bit of pressure to be first, trying to find the **author** or the **press office** for a **comment**. They're also looking at your **competitors'** sites because they want other opinions.

An important *contact* who regularly recommends you is retiring and has appointed their successor. That successor is loyal to a competitor but willing to test both organisations on a level playing field. Right now, they're writing an introductory **email** to you and the competitor to request a **meeting** to discuss a particular project. The successor is looking at both **websites** for evidence to prepare a comparison table.

A key *supplier,* a recruitment consultant, is travelling to your HQ for the annual catch-up, which includes a **presentation**. They have just had interest from a *prize job candidate*. To impress you and demonstrate value at the meeting, they are looking for the latest **news** and **facts and figures** on your **website** to send to the candidate, and they want to arrange a **meeting** before the day is out. In the meantime, the candidate remembers that they know **someone who used to work for your organisation**, so they've arranged to have a drink with them.

This is business as usual. It's beyond your control and happens without you doing a thing. You can't control who comes into your business, or their entry point. But you can control the touchpoints to ensure they have the best possible experience and complete their journeys to a positive conclusion.

The best unmanaged touchpoint I ever unearthed was for a family law firm looking to move into the high-net-worth-individuals market. When we checked the journey, we realised many potential clients (busy people, used to high service levels and who couldn't easily discuss their divorce requirements during the working day) were calling out of hours and getting the answerphone message. This message was over five years old, and the gist of it was 'call back tomorrow when we're open'. Unsurprisingly, there were never any messages.

Finishing touches

- From time to time, step outside of your business and be your own mystery client (do a Brubaker[23]), or employ a professional mystery shopper.

- Look closely at touchpoints where you are losing a large number of people.

- Treat everyone with respect, especially people less fortunate than you who are applying for jobs in your organisation. Think of it as part of your corporate social responsibility.

Now onto connecting and convincing – how to increase your marketing success by avoiding common mistakes.

---

23 *Brubaker* (Twentieth Century-Fox Film Corporation, 1980, directed by Stuart Rosenberg) is a film starring Robert Redford. Redford's character is a prison warden who poses as an inmate in order to clean up the corruption in the prison.

CHAPTER FOUR

How To *Really* Connect And Convince

- Are you and your team busy working on marketing initiatives without knowing, let alone being motivated by, the end game?

- Are you frustrated that the media doesn't use your press releases word-for-word as you provide them?

- Do you open your communications with a statement about how big/established/leading/ unique your organisation is?

- Are you unsure about why your communications aren't working even though they appear to say the right things?

- Do you have a high number of no-shows at your events?

- Do your people find out what's going on in the business after the clients and contacts? (Do the clients and contacts sometimes tell them?)

- Are you puzzled why your communications generated interest but didn't convert to new work?

If you've answered yes to any of these questions, your potential to connect and convince is limited. In this chapter, we look at how to put that right and prepare to succeed in a P2P world.

Have a mission

What gets measured gets done. Starting out with a mission means you're more likely to succeed. I mean an ambitious, active, stretching mission connected to a plan that drives, inspires, and energises your team and keeps you moving forward.

Plan essentials:

- Aims and objectives for the business, for you, and for your team members. These are usually about finance and reputation. As all the best strategists say, begin with the end in mind. You'll need to refer back to this 'end in mind' when you build your Propella grid.

- Measurements, milestones, and your finance and reputation baseline.

- Stakeholders (more on this in a moment).

- Strengths, weaknesses, opportunities, and threats.

- Marketing activity.

- Timetable, resources, and budget.

Know *all* your stakeholders

A stakeholder is someone who can influence the outcome or be influenced by the outcome. Although the range of stakeholders might be broader than you think, the number of people who really matter is smaller. More on that later.

A top-ten starting list of likely stakeholders:

1. Existing and future buyers, clients, and customers

2. Existing and future contacts, multipliers, introducers, referrers, advisers, partners, and third parties

3. Employees and future employees, including any graduates and outsourced staff

4. Existing and future media, influencers, and bloggers

5. Associations, professional bodies, and networks (local, national, international, sector-focused)

6. Local community and neighbours

7. Alumni from all employee levels

8. Competitors, existing and emerging

9. Suppliers and potential suppliers

10. Your lifetime professional and social network

Behind the scenes there are the networks, friends, and families of everybody on the above list. You exist in a web of dependency on people you don't know and will never meet.

There will also be groups within groups whose relevance changes depending on each 'mission'. For example, clients can be categorised by size, income, potential, sector, subsector, location, current and previous work, type of work they buy, and relationship duration. Employees could be further grouped by team, location, status, performance, whether they're employed or outsourced, and length of service.

Write your own list of stakeholders according to a current objective. You'll need it later. At least one of these things will happen:

- You'll be surprised by how many stakeholders you have and how many you never thought of

- You'll realise the massive *existing* potential

- Connections will emerge

- You'll see how both good and bad news can spread quickly

- It'll dawn on you that some people haven't heard from you in a while

Borrow from tried-and-tested communications formulas

Faced with a blank page, or reviewing someone else's draft, borrow from tried-and-tested communications formulas.

- In a news release, the news must be conveyed in five seconds. Subsequent paragraphs should answer who, why, what, where, when, and (my addition) how much; use figures to prove your point.

- In advertising, the formula is AIDA. Use your words to – attract Attention, generate Interest and Desire, prompt some Action.

- Use the think, feel, do framework. This is invaluable. What do you want recipients to think, feel, and do about your communication?

Keep it short. Remember the Mark Twain quote: 'I didn't have time to write a short letter, so I wrote a long one instead.' Imagine you have to pay a £, $, € (or your currency) per word and you'll quickly discover untapped editing skills.

Work the goldmine that is your unique story bank

You will be sitting on a wealth of stories that could bring your work and culture to life. How do you generate, collect, and share your stories inside and outside the business?

Susan Payton, founder of The Business of Stories[24] and an expert in corporate storytelling, in a personal interview for this book, said,

> 'A story is one of the most powerful things that connects us humans. As more and more consumers are making choices based on a brand's mission and vision, telling compelling stories and having a powerful brand narrative is critical.'

She recommends that organisations and their people know and share three stories:

---

24   Susan Payton, 'The Business of Stories'. https://thebusinessofstories. com/.

- Personal story – what led you here, why you do what you do, and why it matters

- Business story – why your business exists, what it stands for, and the difference it makes to the people it serves

- Customer story – where your customer is at, what their story is, and, critically, where *you* fit into *their* story

Think of your story bank as a gold mine in your personalisation toolkit. You can pick stories to match the stakeholder and the situation.

These stories are essential to the next point.

Convert strengths to messages (and prove it)

Your strengths determine your unique messages. Write down the strengths of your offering. Ask others to contribute. Look for answers that share a theme, perhaps about size and strength, and combine them. Convert these strengths into messages. Have at least three primary messages and no more than seven secondary messages.

For each message, have facts, figures, testimonials, or stories to prove the point. This is evidence-based marketing, not the usual guff, and it is incredibly powerful. Then write down the benefit for the stakeholder. Stand in the stakeholder's shoes and ask yourself if it passes the 'so what?' test.

Clive Mieville, Managing Director of international law firm network Mackrell International:

> 'Using this thinking transformed our
> marketing communications. We realised that,
> like so many networks, our communications
> focused on talking to our members, in other
> words, ourselves, and not General Counsel.
> First port of call for most clients is to look at
> our website where now they will see facts,
> figures and client success stories that position
> our network as an attractive alternative
> to a global law firm. They are looking for
> reassurance that we have done this before.
> And, rather than be invisible, we made sure
> our leadership team is in the frontline.'

Avoid the tendency to structure your communication around the school essay formula – introduction, content, conclusion. Instead, start with what the recipient wants to hear or see. Your solution. In his excellent book *rhetorica®: A toolkit of 21 everyday writing techniques*, Scott Keyser recommends this:

'Identify your main message – the one thing you want your reader to take away from your communication. That might be your conclusion, main finding, major insight, chief recommendation, top benefit. Lead with that.'[25]

Choose the right messenger

The 'right' messenger is someone the recipient will respect and not a third party. Busy, successful people receiving your communication will *instantly* judge whether it's worthy of their time based on the sender's credentials.

It's a hierarchy (are you important enough to be worth my time and attention?), tribal (do we share a tribe?), psychological, gut feeling thing.

The messenger must be visible, accountable, and accessible. Can the recipient get hold of the messenger easily, if they want to know more? Indeed, are they encouraged to do so?

The recipient should be able to quickly identify with, like, or admire the messenger. They should feel a connection, or the spark of one.

---

25 S. Keyser, *rhetorica®: A toolkit of 21 everyday writing techniques* (Gorleston: Rethink Press, 2016).

Always factor in gender, generational, and cultural differences.

People choosing a high-value service expect an expert. Being an expert comes with responsibilities, and the first one is authenticity. Clients and targets expect an expert to know *more* than they do, *in depth*, if they are going to add value.

Most messages are intended to be impactful and lead to a successful outcome, so the messenger must look and sound successful and trustworthy.

In a presentation, you have two seconds to make an impact. Those watching will body scan you to decide if you're worthy of their time.

More examples of the 'right' messenger:

- An email or letter announcing major corporate developments should come from the senior partner, not an administrator, database manager, or PR professional

- A campaign to raise a barrister's profile among a specific group of lawyers should come from that barrister, head of chambers, or the practice manager, not an administrator

- An event invitation should be issued by the host or the most senior speaker, not an event manager, an event management company, an event organiser platform, or a PA

It might be attractive, in the short term, to delegate or outsource communications, but you risk limiting your event success. For example, say you're hosting an event and the invitation is issued from someone else or another organisation. Because they might not then value the invitation, the right people will ignore or decline or, worse still, decide not to attend when the time comes. The high volume of no-shows is a great source of frustration for professional firms hosting expensive events.

This leads us on to third parties who can add terrific value, but not where you might think.

Marketing/communications professionals or agencies are brilliant at *facilitating* the marketing and communication, but they shouldn't necessarily front it.

Messengers can sometimes be supported by third-party endorsements, usually from clients or contacts:

- The head of a Family Law team promoting their expertise in challenging cases involving children might include testimonials from clients (anonymous if necessary) who have survived the process.

- An accountancy firm looking to grow their entrepreneurial client base might have videos from real entrepreneurs to showcase the value of their adviser relationship and advice.

- A healthcare lawyer running an event on the latest trends might invite selected and respected sector clients and contacts to form a discussion panel.

Third-party endorsements are especially valuable where there is a generational, cultural, or lifestyle difference between messenger and recipient.

Print, broadcast, and social media are third party for these purposes. Some organisations regard the media as the priority vehicle for communicating their news word-for-word. It's not. The communication should go directly to the recipient and be *supported* by media communications.

Go internal before external

All people in a business should hear about your organisation's news before it goes out externally. There should be a sufficiently robust communications infrastructure and range of tools that allow internal communication to be scheduled first.

Employees can prepare, especially if closely involved. They are more likely to share that news with contacts, clients, friends, family, and their social media network. Test your communications by sharing internally and seeking feedback.

Even if it's a confidential, sensitive issue or a crisis, tell everyone internally first. Whether you tell your people the news a few hours or a few minutes before an external announcement, trust them. They'll trust you in return. And defend you.

If you're concerned about people breaching confidentiality or attacking the organisation (or you personally), then you have a different problem on your hands.

Manage people's progress through the communications journey

Persuading a potential buyer to choose your high-value services takes a lot of hard work (especially if they are loyal elsewhere). Ditto other stakeholders.

The magic moment we're after is when you go to the top of the list, when there's a switch from no to yes – a commitment to your organisation.

The Propella methodology takes stakeholders on a journey:

- Recognition – going from not knowing your name to recognising it

- Reputation – knowing how good you are to choosing you over others

- Recommendation – actively recommending you over competitors

More on this later.

Moving stakeholders along this journey might take hours, days, weeks, months, or years. One communication is never enough. Instead, plan a campaign and maintain it.

Frequency

The intended audience should receive the message in different ways over a period of time, with some intensity at the start. In advertising, this is called OTS, 'Opportunities To See', but it works in all communications.

Decide on frequency with care. There's a fine line between being informative and being a nuisance.

Use big-noise marketing tools to select genuinely interested people (those early and late adopters) and then focus more attention on these people with bespoke events. Say you were launching a new service:

- Stage one – hold a launch event backed by a thought-leadership piece, a before-and-after press release, press coverage, and sponsorship of an industry event with speaker slot, social media, etc.

- Stage two – select interested parties and arrange face-to-face follow-ups with round table events and share exclusive material from the thought-leadership work

Plan well ahead. Double the planning time you've set aside. Enjoy the luxury of being able to do things properly and implement some of the suggestions covered later in the book. Rearrange an event rather than send out late invitations and leave people thinking they're an afterthought.

Timing

Timing is everything in marketing communications. Avoid planning big communications pieces during or around school, national, and religious holidays (because of Christmas, you can forget most of December), major sporting events, and Fridays. Unforeseen occasions include shocking traffic, industrial strikes on transport systems, extreme weather, or a TV drama's climax episode!

Once you factor these things in, there's not a lot of time left for your communication to hit the spot.

Sometimes, timing is predetermined (e.g. say by annual results or sector events). If timing is determined by a planned or unplanned news item, be among the first to roll out your campaign or communications but never last. James Goldsmith's quote 'If you see a bandwagon, it's too late' definitely applies here.

Timing must work for the recipient, not the sender. My favourite Larry Hochman quote makes a brilliant point: 'Customers want your products or your services, not at the speed of light, but at the speed of life, their life.'[26]

Find your voice

In professional services, there is an established norm, which means that organisations tend to look and sound the same. Personalise that norm.

People buy from people, so be yourself. Scott Keyser writes: 'In business, where everyone is clamouring to be heard in a crowded marketplace, companies that express a strong point of view in an authentic, human voice are more likely to be listened to.'[27]

Avoid the temptation to leave your personality at the door. Connect with your tone of voice and use it.

---

26 Hochman, *The Relationship Revolution*.
27 Keyser, *rhetorica®*.

Keyser says: 'We don't read tone of voice; we hear it. When we strike a tone of voice that makes our reader feel good about us and the content, they're more receptive to our message.'[28]

Use adult-to-adult language and don't be needy.

Avoid clichés: 'Hope you are well.' 'I am delighted.' 'Reach out.' If you wouldn't say that to someone in person, don't write it to them. These vacuous phrases destroy authenticity.

Acknowledge different learning types

People absorb information according to their dominant learning preference. The three most common are visual, auditory, or kinaesthetic (see Neil Fleming's VAK model[29]). Busy people (that's everyone) skim-read communications and absorb messages received in their dominant learning style.

Visual people like to *see* things. Pictures (thank you whoever invented infographics), charts, diagrams, video, and Mind Maps® offer colourful, bright representations of your message.

---

28 Keyser, *rhetorica*®.
29 For more on Neil Fleming's VAK or VARK learning styles, google 'learning styles'.

Auditory people like to *hear* things. They process words in a way that creates links in their brains – think conversations, phone calls, webinars, brainstorming, meetings, video blogs, presentations, and events.

Kinaesthetic people like to *do* things. They want to *feel* if it's right for them. They warm to messages that are filled with action words and energy levels that engage passion, conversation, and interaction.

The temptation is to deliver communications in a way that suits you, the sender. Too frequently, this means communication that is data-heavy, filled with information that, while accurate and interesting to the sender, is not compelling for the recipient.

Not understanding these differences must be what prompted George Bernard Shaw to say that 'the biggest problem with communication is the illusion it has taken place.'

Instead, use well-chosen words in your communications to appeal to each VAK type.

In an interview for this book, Paul Richmond, keynote speaker and managing director of the Grogroup said:

> 'To engage their audience and embed key
> messages, good presenters and facilitators,
> the ones in demand that leave their mark on

an audience, go to great lengths to ensure that their sessions are rich in diverse language and techniques to appeal to every preference.'[30]

Balance convenience with impact

Convenience comes down to time and money: how easily can its distribution be delegated without compromising the sender's integrity, taking up time, and costing money?

Impact comes down to how likely it is that the communication will engage the recipient? Will it move them along that communications journey?

Examples of high convenience but low impact and high impact but low convenience:

- Email is a highly convenient form of communication, but its ubiquity means low impact.

- A handwritten (or hand-signed) letter or phone call will have a massive impact, but neither is terribly convenient because they take time.

- The blog, the Tweet, and the LinkedIn update might be easy to send out. Someone else can

---

30   Paul Richmond can be contacted by email: paul@thegrogroup.com.

even do it for you. But they risk being lost in the background noise so are potentially low impact.

- Phoning a few people to let them know what you're doing in advance might take time but will generate enormous impact.

Avoid automatically choosing the most convenient tool to you. Instead, choose a range of tools right for the occasion, the person, and the time. You can also top up the impact by using personalisation techniques covered in Chapter 13. There are plenty of communications tools that are convenient *and* generate impact.

Finish with a call to action

Always include what you want people to do as a result of seeing your communication. That might be:

- Visit a website
- Call someone
- Meet someone
- Ask something
- Apply for something
- Download something

- Follow something

- Like, share, or comment on something

A call to action kick-starts momentum, filters genuine interest, and provides early measurement of interest.

Always invite feedback. Communication is a two-way process. Otherwise, it's just 'telling'.

Preparation complete.

Now we move on to where the magic starts to happen. And the fun.

SECTION 3
PROPELLA EXPLAINED – PLOT, PRIORITISE, AND PLAN

(Where the magic starts to happen; we're going deep into Propella thinking.)

Warning – mindset change required

All people are important, but some are more important to you and your business than others. You need to choose who is important for different goals.

Remember, Propella sits at the unexplored intersection of personalisation and technology. Propella represents the best of the past (good manners, being human), the present (technology), and the future (more technology).

Propella methodology means you can:

- **Plot** your unique stakeholder landscape by groups, organisations, and people

- **Prioritise** these groups, organisations, and people

- **Plan** your marketing and communications approach according to the priority level of groups, organisations, and people

- **Personalise** your marketing and communications for your priority groups, organisations, and people

Propella business intelligence software is a digital version of the analogue grid-based stakeholder map used in marketing, communications, and management training (but often stays, unexploited, in the training folder on the office shelf).

Propella business intelligence software gives you a dynamic, tangible, working, real-time, updatable version of your own map (or maps). You can share your thinking with others to encourage the pooling of vital market, organisation, and people intelligence. Team members can be allocated responsibility for managing designated groups, organisations, and people. You monitor progress by moving group, organisation, and people icons on the screen as you develop the relationships. The reporting system provides measurements and a format to share progress. Here is a currency for your relationship capital.

The Client and Markets Director of a top-50 law firm used Propella to unite a newly merged corporate team:

> 'The Propella methodology works so well with teams – by working through the various steps together, there's an unseen commitment to helping each other win new clients and deepen existing client relationships. At the start of the day, we had a group of individuals – at the end of the day, we had a team with a common purpose and common language.'

However, you don't need the software to apply the Propella principles we're about to cover.

Why does it work?

Propella gives you a structure – a road-map for managing marketing communications. With clarity on your priorities, you and your team know where to invest your time, energy, and money.

Jenny Hardy, Strategic Development Director at WLG Gowling:

> 'The beauty of Propella is that it forces you to work out who really matters. Yes, it requires time and thought upfront, but that investment is richly rewarded: clarity on the people who can (and can't) make a difference to your business, a failsafe method for allocating resources, budget and time, and effective results from your communications activities.'

The investment you make in this process *will* deliver results. Sometimes these results are achieved quickly, with the smallest of gestures, and cost nothing. Progress is visible and will encourage you to do more. It works for right-brained and left-brained people. Finance directors respond positively to Propella's logic because resources are well spent and ROI is managed.

© marketoonist.com

Rachel Maguire, CEO at Arko Iris, a specialist investor relations consultancy, sums it up: 'Propella takes the touchy-feely and makes it into the quantifiable. In a world where what gets measured gets done, Propella's forensic approach will help you find growth and measurable results.'

It works for extroverts and introverts. For extroverts, it's a solid platform to measure the outcome of activity. Introverts need never 'sell' again. Propella is a comfortable system to use because it encourages you to be your authentic self.

Its application is serious. The future of your organisation might depend on it. But it's also fun to use. Light-bulb moments come thick and fast, and I've seen plenty of people laugh out loud when they discover an easy opportunity. How many marketing plans or awaydays have ever given that pleasure?

On the back of a confident rebranding, St Ives Chambers wanted to reposition its offer around high-quality work and a friendly approach backed by essential critical mass.

Elizabeth Isaacs, QC of St Ives Chambers:

'Encouraging barristers to work in teams and engage in marketing is no easy task but we succeeded by using this system. It helped us transform the approach of members and clerks to growing the practice by taking the fear out of marketing and business development. The different practice teams united behind a shared direction and it unlocked individual potential to look after our clients.'

Think of Propella as a team game you play to win.

CHAPTER FIVE
Gathering The Information

Download time.

Revisit your mission, picture of success, aims and objectives, or goals. Record the factors behind your decision and note deadlines and milestones. Think now about your most active, annoying, and/or admired competitors. This reasoning will become clear when I explain how to outmanoeuvre those competitors.

Gather the information to inform your decisions. In Edward de Bono's 'Six Thinking Hats' language, this is White Hat territory – 'The facts, just the facts.'[31]

---

31 E. de Bono, *Six Thinking Hats* (New York, Little Brown and Company, 1985).

Going through this process, *which you can revisit and update,* allows you to challenge any assumptions you may have made about the market and work sources. This is also a perfect opportunity to check for new data and ensure you can constantly keep abreast of emerging information. Subsequent decisions and activity will be far more robust.

You'll need to gather information from internal and external sources. Popular places to start:

- Top-billing clients by turnover and profitability, including historic data showing changing trends and which services these clients buy.

- Industry, sector, or country research/reports from governments, associations, media, organisations, and whatever else has informed your decisions.

- What exists in your head (rarely do I see clients refer to their CRM systems) and in the heads of your team. Propella works best when used with a team because intelligence is 'pooled' and everyone works towards a shared goal. In my experience, it's the intelligence people keep in their heads, not recorded anywhere, that proves to be the most useful.

- Information about work sources, including introducers and referrals. If this isn't recorded, think about it now.

- Marketing information, including website data, attendance at events, responses to direct mail, pitches won and lost, client-service interviews, and conversations with stakeholders.

If you don't have the facts, it's fine to rely on your gut feeling until you can confirm your thoughts.

Propella starts with the big picture, your big picture, and then gets down to relevant granularity. Effort invested here provides a channel for your ambition and will save you time later.

Get your thinking cap on. Grab a piece of paper. Open a new page in your notebook or tablet. If you use them, start a new Mind Map®. Order strong coffee. Or put the kettle on. Note that you may need cake…

Focus on one 'mission' or project at a time. By the end of this section, you'll have something, diagrammatically, that looks like Fig 5.1.

The Propella process will shift your focus away from what you have to sell and onto what organisations and people want to buy.

- You'll know at the macro level exactly which stakeholder groups will deliver your success, one goal at a time.

Groups

Organisations

People

Fig 5.1 Organising your thinking might look like the Propella project system, where you add the names.

- You'll know the names of some organisations within those groups (the rest will come later).

- You'll know the names or job titles of some people within those organisations.

Gathering the information – the groups

Most Propella users start with the macro level and, one group at a time (this is important or the whole task will become overwhelming), users almost immediately break the overall group down into subgroups. Group your stakeholders based on how they see themselves. Users can also categorise them again by applying other criteria, including world location, country by region, or size based on turnover, number of employees, or position in league tables.

Think of this level as the foundation. Once it's laid, you can build the other grids and moving through them will be a flow. Users then move through organisations, one group at a time, and then people, one organisation at a time.

Here's a list of popular generic groups with some recent client examples.

- Industry or business sectors and subsectors

  □ Education sector in England – universities, higher education, further education, state schools, independent schools, early years, support services

  □ Venture capitalists – fund size, specialist interest, established more than ten years/less than ten years

  □ Law firms and chambers with arbitration capability – UK only, Europe only, worldwide

- Company or organisation types filtered by size in terms of turnover, growth rates, people numbers, location, sector, policies

  □ Listed/private companies in the retail sector, UK HQ or office, outlets up to 10/10 to 20/20 – 30/30 – 40/40 – 50/more than 50, international/Europe only

  □ Organisations, public or private sector, with more than 250 employees in a specific geographic region

  □ Fastest-growing companies by industry sector and region

  □ UK law firms by partner size (2 to 20/20 – 40/40 – 60/60 – 80/80-100/more than 100)

- Other professional firms, contacts, referrers

  - Accountancy firms with designated Healthcare team further divided by location in the world

  - Top 100 UK law firms without private-client service offering

  - UK's top 100 architect partnerships, UK or overseas-income dominated, commercial or private work reputation

- People 'types' or roles grouped in the criteria relevant to your mission

  - HR directors at FTSE 350, UK based with global responsibility, location by UK region

  - Head of in-house legal, public sector, size of team (more or less than 50)

  - Entrepreneurs, gender, technology/non-technology, VC or non-VC backed

Your organisation, your place in your chosen sector, and your ambition are unique to you. The trigger questions below are intended to stimulate your thinking rather than be a prescriptive final list.

- What groups and subgroups have worked well in the past?

- What groups give you work, income, profit?

- What are you famous for and where?

- What do you want to be famous for and where?

- Where is the money?

- What groups have the potential to grow?

- Which emerging groups resonate with you and your business?

- What about supplier groups?

- What about community groups?

Include your own organisation as a group.

Have at least one but no more than twenty groups on one map. As you get going, you're likely to have several maps at group level.

Thinking about historic work sources can reveal surprising results. Clients often realise they have neglected rich work sources. My two favourites are the Wills and Trusts team who realised a significant percentage of good quality work came from one funeral director, and the Family Law team who identified one counsellor at an independent rehab clinic as a prolific work provider. Using Propella, both firms went on to develop stronger referral relationships with *more* people at both organisations and similar people in *other* organisations. Other productive sources are alumni, competitors (especially if referring the work to you means they aren't giving work to a bigger competitor), and clients previously on the 'other side'.

At this point, Propella users with the option can request (or nominate!) volunteers, preferably those with a connection to the mission, to take responsibility for a specific group. Some skin in the game is always an advantage. I'm amazed by what happens when you give people a 'mission' rather than a 'task' – that's semantics for you. In my experience, people (even the most cynical about 'marketing') respond positively to this for several reasons. The focus of responsibility is defined, and the goal is clear and manageable. People also respond well to the competitive element. They enjoy a) beating external competitors and b) outperforming colleagues on whatever mission they've been assigned. Accordingly, they are also responsible for the organisations and people within the group.

Gathering the information – the organisations

Focusing on *one* group or subgroup at a time, starting with the most important, write down the names of the organisations within that group.

Use this list to prompt your thinking:

- Existing and future clients
- Existing and future contacts, multipliers, introducers, referrers, advisers, and third parties

- Internal teams, departments, jobs roles, or office location

- Existing and future media publications

- Associations, professional bodies, and networks (local, national, international, sector-focused)

- Local community and neighbours

- Alumni – any particular role, organisation, or location

- Competitors, existing and emerging

- Suppliers and potential suppliers

- Your lifetime professional and social network

You can (and will) go back for more organisations later.

Gathering the information – the people

Focusing on *one* organisation at a time, starting with the one that matters most, write down all the people you know and then all the people you *should* know who can help you achieve your goal. At this stage, you might have some job titles instead of real names.

Here's a popular, but far from comprehensive, role list to prompt your thinking:

- Head of in-house legal/General Counsel plus team members and specialists

- Finance Director plus team members and specialists

- Head of HR, team members, and specialists

- Board director, board members, and non-executives

- Managing Director, business owner, founder

- Senior partner, managing partner, head of team

- Editor, journalist, reporter, blogger, influencer, researcher

- Recruitment consultant

Colleagues and employees are very important here. You might depend on an internal colleague, employee, or group to support your goal, provide an internal service, or pave the way. Internal people may also be connected to someone you want to know externally. That 'two degrees of separation' rule could mean that somebody will know somebody who can introduce you to someone you want to know.

When I brainstorm this in groups, the often astonishing discovery (to participants) is that the most promising and even immediate work potential comes through people *in* the business or through existing contacts (in, say, a membership association). The first most memorable discovery was made by an employment head looking, rather urgently, to increase the amount of work received from the UK's major employers – comprising over 10,000 employees – and whose immediate request was for coverage in an HR magazine – the wrong solution for the problem. Using Propella, we worked out that his own client partners could provide direct access to at least ten of those employers. The second most memorable discovery was made by an accountancy practice looking to increase its international entrepreneur client base. Using this process, the partners realised they enjoyed instant access to 120 of their counterparts through the firm's international association membership.

One advantage of doing this work in groups or consulting with others is the sharing and pooling of contacts. My favourite laugh-out-loud-told-you-this-would-work moment happened while working with the head of a Litigation team who couldn't get through to a significant person in a target client's legal team. After the request had been shared, one junior person piped up and said that they'd been to university with this person and could easily make the introduction!

My laugh-out-loud-I-cannot-believe-my-luck moment happened after I'd spent a frustrating few weeks trying to help a client get through to a pivotal person in a local authority. The client and I went out to a restaurant only to find that we were sat next to this pivotal person. We knew it was him because

we'd done our homework and knew what he looked like from
a website photograph. He was alone. There was no escape. He
actually enjoyed the interaction. Amazing what happens when
you focus on the right person.

Looking back to the education sector example on page
88.

Groups – Education would be the main group, and
universities would be a subgroup further grouped by
type of university (e.g. Russell Group, Alliance universities, private universities).

Organisations – Each group has designated member
universities, plus there are associations for each, along
with specialist media.

People – Every university will have easy-to-find
decision-makers. Each association will have named
contacts, and each media outlet will have named specialist reporters.

Most examples throughout this book relate to winning
business from existing or new clients. This methodology also works for:

- Effective crisis management (I even used it to
  good effect on one last minute occasion when
  journalists were about to break a nightmare-
  scenario story)

- Accelerating internal cross-selling programmes

- Selecting and approaching external merger candidates

- Deciding which external conferences, networking events, and speaking opportunities to attend and awards to pursue

- Efficient event management to increase the number of right-profile attendees and to reduce costs and dropouts

- Accelerating change management programmes

- Recruiting best-fit graduates

- Coaching individuals who need to improve relationships with key people

Told you that you'd need cake.

In this chapter, we've looked at the information you need to start using the Propella grid. You started with groups that mattered most to your success. You've noted some organisations that matter within those groups. And you're now thinking about the people who matter to your success in some of those chosen organisations. Now you're ready to start plotting.

CHAPTER SIX

Propella Explained (Part One)

You know where you're going. You know how quickly you want to get there. And based on some macro-level groups, you have the names of some organisations and people who could influence your outcome.

Now it's time to determine where to focus your best effort on the Propella grid. Fig 6.1 is a naked version so you can see where you're going.

In this chapter, I'm going to show you how to build your grid.

Fig 6.1 The naked Propella grid

100 🩶

Nicola Mumford, former London managing partner of Wragge & Co (now Gowling WLG):

> 'This is the most succinct, easy to remember and practical methodology for articulating what you want of your client base that I've ever used. Once the grid is set, the instructions and direction of travel are crystal clear. The sole aim is to move the right people into a place where they are recommending you internally and externally.'

Once you get going, you'll have multiple grids for different objectives. In fact, once you get going, you'll just plot people automatically.

The grid can be scaled up for major projects and big-picture goals or scaled down for teams or events. Over time, you can build a portfolio of Propella grids. If you have a big enough team, you can allocate responsibility for individual Propella grid management to different people.

Start with the Royalty axis, then the Loyalty axis. All of your groups, organisations, and people will end up with two numbers between 0 and 100. These numbers determine where they should appear on the Propella grid and what treatment they should be given.

To avoid being overwhelmed, for each mission, approach Propella in this order:

1. Plot your groups and subgroups.

2. Plot the organisations of the most important group. You'll see why once you get going.

3. Plot the people of your top three most important organisations.

4. Work through the rest of the organisations.

5. Work through the people.

6. At this point, most Propella users realise they have plenty to be getting on with, decide to implement the next stage and come back for the next group later.

7. Go back to the next most important group and start again.

There is no need to rush. This is not a quick fix. Getting this foundation right takes time.

Please stick with it.

Plotting groups

Royalty axis – value, influence, power

The vertical Royalty axis is about value, influence, and power. Consider the groups you've written down. What is the size and potential of their spending on whatever it is you're offering? Is this sector increasing or decreasing in size or value? It's also about kudos, existing and potential, say of working with a dynamic or prestigious group.

At the group level, you're looking to identify who has the most power and value to meet your particular need. This might change depending on your objective. On a scale of 0 to 100, how important is this group to your outcome?

Those with the most power sit at the top of the axis and the grid (see Fig 6.2). The visual learners among you will respond to how these extremes are illustrated (with a fool's cap and a crown).

Criteria for choosing groups, organisations, and people are unique to every business and those making the decisions. You have complete flexibility regarding which criteria to apply.

To get going, start with the extremes. Select your most important group and your least important one and assign them numbers on the axis. Then assign numbers to the others. What's really important is to decide whether they'll sit above or below 50.

Anything and anybody above the 50 line is going to be significant to your future.

If you're not sure, you might put them at 49, 50, or 51 – their true place will emerge later. Adjusting the numbers is normal.

To start with, most Propella users base the 50 line on the spending capacity the groups, organisations, or people have for their services. When deciding on the 50 line I call it setting the co-ordinates, but you can change these at any time.

Loyalty axis – recognition, reputation, recommendation

On this horizontal axis, we measure knowledge, buy-in, or advocacy levels to your organisation. This is the communications journey we covered earlier – moving groups, organisations, and people along a journey from recognition to recommendation. What is the status of your relationship with a particular group? The visual cues for the extremes are a love heart and a broken heart (see Fig 6.3).

Fig 6.2 Who is valuable, powerful, and influential and who is not. The Royalty axis with clear division line at 50. You choose.

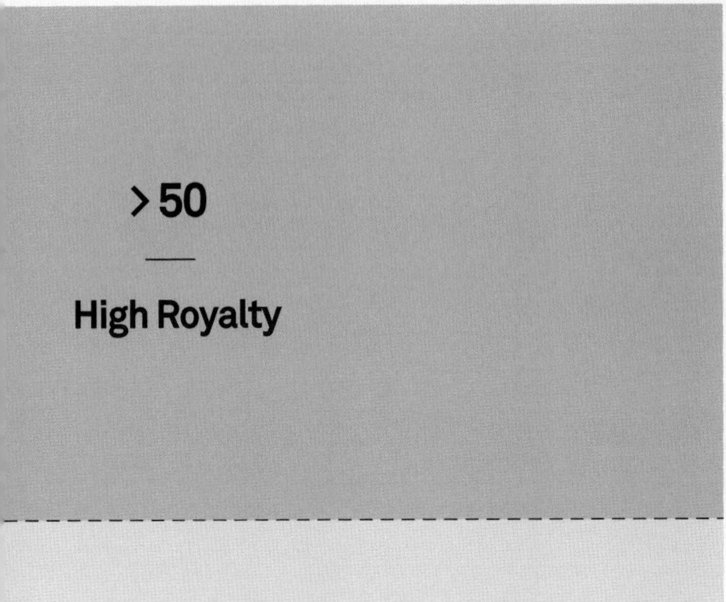

> 50

—

High Royalty

< 50

—

Low Royalty

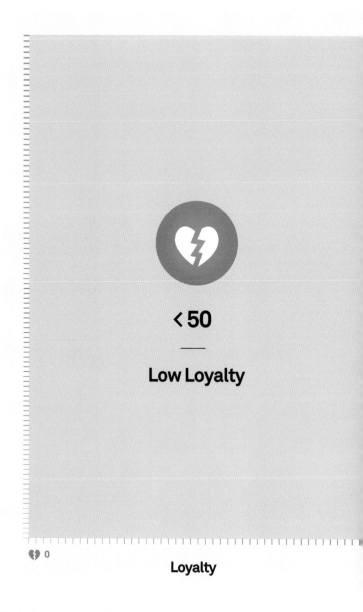

Fig 6.3 Who is loyal to you with income, market share, introductions, or coverage? The Loyalty axis with clear division line at 50. You decide.

Recognition – Zero recognition is the starting point, on the far left. How much work do you have from this group? What's your market share?

Reputation – The halfway point. Does this group know about your reputation? Are they giving you some of their work but not all of it?

Recommendation – On the right. Are you so highly regarded by this group that you are openly recommended by organisations within the group or by an association representing the group? Your market share is high.

Starting with the most important group on your Royalty axis, assign this group a number on the Loyalty axis. Do the same for your least important group. Consider what percentage of total income you generate from each group – think of 100 as where you have the largest possible market share. How well known are you in this sector or geographic location? Even at this stage, the ambitious among you will be thinking and feeling what it would be like to plot your most important group on the far right of the Loyalty axis. This will help you plot the group's current position.

Once you get started, the group positions will fall into place.

- **0** – No traction (you aren't earning any income from anyone in this group and there's zero recognition)

- **0–25** – Limited traction (still no income or influence, slight reputation)

- **25–50** – Some traction (and getting interesting)

- **50–75** – Looking good (you're well known in this sector)

- **75–99** – About as good as it gets (you're generating substantial income from this group and recognised as a leader in this field)

- **100** – The Holy Grail (you're the dominant player in this group)

When you finish, you'll have two numbers for each group and can place the groups on the grid.

It will look something like Fig 6.4, which was created for a client considering which sector groups to invest in.

Now that you've got your group picture, you can plot the organisations.

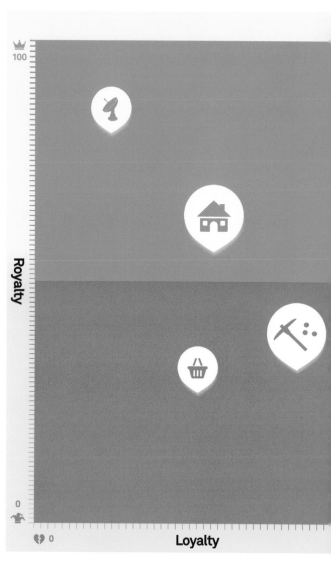

 **Groups**

Fig 6.4 Propella showing the value and loyalty of sector groups

Organisations

On a new grid, plot the organisations according to Royalty (how important they are to you) and Loyalty (how loyal they are to you). Again, it's useful to start with the most and least important organisations on your list. This will help you establish the 50 dividing line. Remember, you can alter the numbers later. Choose your own criteria.

Royalty – For clients, targets, income sources, and contacts, you're assessing their place on the axis according to factors such as spend, potential spend, size, status, kudos, ambition, confidence, success, ownership, stability, environmental and ethics policies, and reputation. Most users start with how important each organisation is based on spend and its percentage of total turnover. A less common but valuable criterion is payment record. Likeability is also important. For influencers, including the media and industry associations, you might think about size, reach, quality, and followers. For suppliers, think about how critical they are to your business. What internal teams do you need to achieve your goal?

Decide on the number between 0 and 100.

Loyalty – How much is your firm recognised by this organisation? At 0 they don't know you exist. Moving towards 25 they may have heard of you. At 25 to 50 they're aware of you but have not yet given you any work. For most users, an organisation crosses the 50 line when they move from target to client and, at some point in the last twelve months, an invoice has been issued to that organisation. If it's a media publication, do they sometimes include you but it's not a foregone conclusion and you have to do all the chasing? Then we move towards the 100 point of recommendation – by the time you're heading towards 100, this organisation will be giving you most if not all of the work and openly recommending you. This will be a fairly exclusive relationship, and price is never an issue. If it's a media publication they always come to you for comment and you are likely to be receiving a lot of positive coverage. Internal teams will be giving you their full support, making you a priority.

Decide on the number between 0 and 100.

You'll now have two numbers for this organisation and can plot it on the grid.

The result will look something like Fig 6.5, which demonstrates relevant organisations for a firm wanting to sell a specific service line into the banking sector.

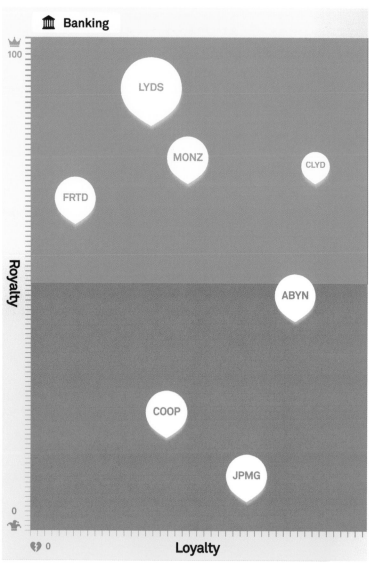

 Organisations

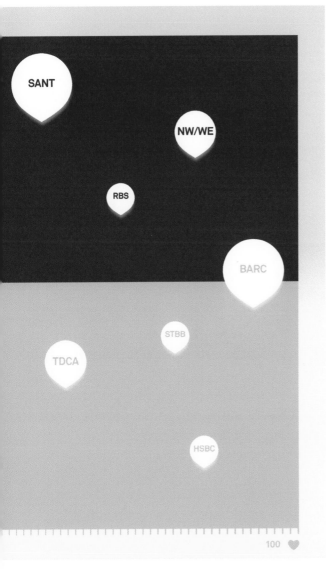

Fig 6.5 Drilling down from group to organisations, this is how it looked for a client selling a service line into the banking sector.

People

Start a new people grid for each organisation and plot the people you know and want to know. Royalty first. Start with extremes – the most powerful and the least powerful for your purposes. Power *within* an organisation usually refers to status, seniority, knowledge, or responsibility. You'll be looking at buying power, the board, the decision-makers, the policymakers, the gatekeepers. The external influencers could include advisers, journalists, high-profile sector experts, association spokespeople, and bloggers.

Internal people might be key team and board members, other individuals with access to your clients and targets, business-services professionals, and all those managing your touchpoints. Give each person a number between 0 and 100 that reflects their Royalty value relevant to your goal.

Now Loyalty. Choose a number on the Loyalty axis for this person using the three Rs to guide you, recognition, reputation, recommendation.

- **0** – You have no traction with this person. If asked about you, they would say, 'I've never heard of them.'

- **0–25** – Limited traction (still no income or influence, slight reputation). If asked about you, they would say, 'I know the name, but I don't know anyone there', or 'We don't give them any work because they don't do what we want.'

- **25–50** – Some traction (and getting interesting). If asked about you, they would say, 'I've looked at them but haven't given them any work', or 'We've given them a bit of work but…', or 'Yes, I've heard of them and I think they're quite good, worth a look.'

The 50 line is critical because, as you'll see in the next chapter, it will determine how you're going to communicate with the person in the future. Above the 50 line I would expect them to be giving you work, profile, introductions, loyalty, support – how much they're giving you will determine where they sit between 50 and 100.

- **50–75** – Looking good (you're well known to this person who is giving you plenty of work). If asked about you, they would say, 'They're very good, top ten in this field. We rate them but we don't give them everything.'

- **75–100** – About as good as it gets (you're generating substantial income from this person). If asked about you, they would say, 'Oh yes, they really are very good indeed, excellent reputation. They would be in my top three for what you're after.' The longer you've known a person, the more likely they are to be at the top end of the Loyalty axis.

- **100** – The Holy Grail (you're the clear leader for this person in your chosen group; there's a marked distance between you and the next competitor). If asked about you, they would say, 'They're brilliant. I know them really well. Honestly the best in the market. They set the pace for others to follow. Don't go anywhere else – tell you what, I'll give you the name of the person you should get in touch with and the direct line. Tell them I sent you.'

In the rare event that one of your chosen priority people says, 'Can't stand that organisation. Not to be trusted. They won't last', they go to a negative place on the Loyalty axis. We have plans for this person later.

When you finish, you'll have two numbers and can place the person on the grid.

At this stage, many users realise that they have good relationships with some, but not all, of the right people, and that their relationship with the organisation is not as secure or future-proofed as they would like.

You'll end up with a people grid that looks like Fig 6.6, this fictitious example for Santander. Note the option for male and female figures. Important.

Now that there are groups, organisations, and people in the grid quadrants, we'll look at what those quadrants mean and what to do with them.

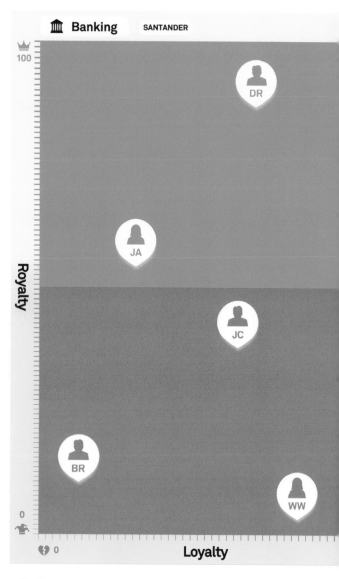

 People

Fig 6.6 This is how Propella looks at the people level within one organisation. We use initials to identify them and male/female icons.

CHAPTER SEVEN

Propella Explained (Part Two)

Now that you have your bespoke grids, here's the ideal communications approach for each quadrant (see Fig 7.1):

1. VIPs – partner with/wow

2. Upgraders – find the common ground/woo

3. Standard – keep them informed

4. No Frills – tell them

Most organisations communicate with all their stakeholders using the standard approach; they keep them informed by pushing out large volumes of commoditised marketing.

Fig 7.1 Propella with named quadrants that each merit a specific marketing communications approach.

100 ♥

125

High Royalty, high Loyalty – VIPs

VIPs are those groups, organisations, or people in the grid's top-right quadrant.

Characteristics:

- On a macro level, this is a worthwhile group where you're already well known.

- On an organisational level, your VIPs are likely to be existing clients giving you work. The further along the Loyalty axis they are, the more work they'll be giving you. Referrers are handing you good introductions and those on the far right in this quadrant are passing you their best. A media publication is giving you good profile, or well-connected influencers are sharing some of your news. The further to the right they are, the more they're talking about you. Internally these are your higher-performing, reliable teams.

- On a people level, they are decision-makers, the players, senior team, the C-suite, the ones who count. They know about your reputation and those on the quadrant's far right are actively recommending you. They attend your events and reply to your communications. You're a top three for the referrers in this box, and the further to the right of the grid they are, the more likely they are to choose you and look after your interests in their organisation. These are the journalists who always come to you as the authority. Internally, they might be the important people you can count on for support when you're trying to achieve something. You look forward to seeing these people. In a crisis, they are who you would trust, take into your confidence, and rely on to help you through it.

Partnering with your VIPs will help to accelerate your mission. VIPs are the only stakeholder group with whom you should *consult*. They make great sounding boards and are ideal for sense-checking an idea or initiative (and early buy-in is secured at the same time).

Partnering means working together and *being seen* to work together.

- Externally – On your website, you name them, have an endorsement from them, or perhaps discuss them in a case study. They might speak at a client or internal event, or you could share a platform at a relevant industry event to show people you're a pair. Your organisation may have visibility on their website.

- Internally – You involve them in meetings, ask them to cascade news or information, give them a shared platform at internal events, and give them internal profile.

The VIPs are your number one priority. You need to wow them, impress them, delight them, and knock their socks off, day in and day out. Work for VIPs is always your very best, and your marketing communications to this group should be personalised.

If you feel uncomfortable about partnering with them, they're probably in the wrong place on the grid.

The aim of all your marketing and communications is to create and keep as many VIPs as possible.

Are you beginning to see how your monthly news roundup, the standard invitation to your showcase event, or a posted copy of your annual report is a wasted opportunity to hit the spot with your VIPs?

If you do only one thing after reading this book, look after your VIPs.

High Royalty, low Loyalty – Upgraders

Upgraders are the groups, organisations, or people in the top-left quadrant. These are your *potential* VIPs, but their loyalty is directed elsewhere.

They are highly valuable, influential, and/or powerful in relation to your goal, but they don't know you well enough. Not yet, anyway, but we'll come to that.

Characteristics:

- At the macro level, these are valuable or powerful groups where you want more work and to build your reputation.

- On an organisational level, they will be your targets, multipliers who think you are unimportant, media outlets where you have yet to have any coverage, and industry associations who have not heard of you. People in this quadrant will be the influential and powerful within those organisations, top journalists, or opinion formers for the sector. Internally, they might be people you need to achieve your goal but who are not on your side as much as they should be.

- In recruitment terms, they might be a key person you want in your organisation.

With Upgraders, the communications approach is to **find the common ground**. What do they want or need that you've got or can help them with?

You're **wooing** them, day in and day out. You're showing them what it *feels* like to be a client, contact, or an employee. You're making them feel special, giving them a taste of the VIP treatment.

Are you beginning to see how your 'sales' calls, mass brochure mailings, and social media campaigns are missing the mark with these people?

Your mission is to convert these Upgraders into your VIPs. If you use the grid properly, you'll soon have the names and numbers of the people you need to reach. Your marketing and communications from now on will rise above the noise and be absolutely focused and bespoke.

The bonus points come thick and fast for those who partner with their VIPs to *convert* the Upgraders.

Low Royalty, high Loyalty – Standard

Standard is in the bottom-right quadrant.

Characteristics:

- At a macro level, these are groups who like your organisation but have low spending levels, are in decline, or no longer aligned with your goals.

- It could be a client you have outgrown, or one overtaken by their competitors. Sometimes these are clients who spend small amounts of money and take up a disproportionate amount of time. Your association with them is not helping your reputation. You are at different places in your respective hierarchies and the mismatch is too great. Quite simply, they just don't have what you want or need to achieve your objective, but their association with you is good for *them*.

- At a people level, they could be people working in referrers who don't have the right contacts for your goal so can't give you the introductions you want, but their association with you is good for *their* reputation. A regular in this box is a local or insignificant media publication who pesters you for advertising and sponsorship.

They could even be your mates. It's easy and even pleasurable to spend time with those in this group. I've had some clients who confess to having family in this quadrant. And there's an 'obligation'. Unfortunately, it won't contribute to your goal and will divert your resources away from the priority VIPs and Upgraders.

The communications approach here is to **keep them informed**.

Your regular one-size-fits-all communications are enough to meet their needs. There is no need to invest large sums of money or time. You can keep on broadcasting your news to this group and there is no time pressure.

It's worth keeping a careful eye on selected people in this group, especially those in the top of the quadrant, in case they move up into the VIP camp. A sector or subsector might suddenly have a new lease of life and be positioned for growth. At an organisational level, a small client might be taken over by a larger organisation which appears in your VIPs or Upgraders quadrant (smart Propella operators will have foreseen that opportunity and orchestrated it). At a people level, it could be the junior person who is promoted, takes over during a sabbatical or maternity cover, or moves into a senior position elsewhere.

Low Royalty, low Loyalty – No Frills

The No Frills is in the bottom-left quadrant. At a macro level, these are groups in decline who aren't valuable or important to you and, thankfully, aren't interested in you either. These groups don't emerge until you realise who *is* valuable, important, and powerful – your VIPs and Upgraders. At an organisational level, they might be clients you no longer work for – and they're unlikely to be clients again – because they don't have the work you want. That said, look out for people in these organisations who recognise that they need to move on and could transfer to a VIP or Upgrader business. Occasionally they are former Upgraders who were once worth pursuing but are no longer in your line of sight (and you were never in theirs) because things have changed. Regular candidates in this quadrant are companies in crisis or dealing with debt (so not good for business unless, of course, you're selling crisis management, recovery, or funding services); poor payers; and once promising organisations who didn't follow advice previously given. Other signs to look out for are justified negative news coverage, accusations of fraud and wrongdoing, facing volume or large-scale litigation, sudden and/or *en masse* departure of senior people (especially respected individuals), high employee turnover, and poor satisfaction ratings on employment websites. Within the media they are fringe (even bogus) publications or small-time influencers. These things can happen at any time. Yet still they receive your newsletters and invitations to your showcase events. They may even appear on your public client list. At a people level, they might be directors or employees in these organisations, journalists and sales people for fringe publications, or poor-performing and disinterested employees.

You might realise that colleagues and employees are spending a disproportionate amount of time with No Frills organisations and people.

That said, keep an eye on those in the top of the No Frills quadrant. You can put an arrow on them if you think they might possibly head upwards.

The communications approach is to **tell them** what's happening, or even what's happened. Broadcast media is fine – they can pick it up if they want it. They don't merit any special attention.

A few words on Propella and data protection

Propella was designed to a) minimise inappropriate and excessive marketing to individuals; and b) improve the marketing experience by personalisation. However, users in the UK and Europe must take care to adhere to GDPR around the holding and processing of personal information of individuals. Any information must be used in compliance with data protection laws relevant to individual countries.

Sally Mewies, Technology and Data partner at Gowling WLG, highlights some of the GDPR areas you need to be aware of when using Propella.

- Marketing needs to be carried out lawfully and there are additional rules for unsolicited electronic direct marketing.

- Personal data includes anything that identifies someone – name, email address, phone number. Comply with all the data protection principles, including processing in a fair and transparent manner. Typically this will be covered in a privacy notice on your website.

- Keep a record of the purpose for which the contact details were initially collected. Personal data can be used only for the purposes for which it was collected. In the case of Propella, that purpose is likely to be marketing and business development.

- You need to have a 'legal ground' for processing personal data. If you are following the principles in this book then the legal ground for processing is likely to be a legitimate interest one, i.e. it is in your legitimate interests to develop business. You may need consent as well, depending on the type of marketing you're doing.

- Make sure you provide mechanisms to keep information up to date. Personal information needs to be accurate and not kept for longer than necessary.

- Do not keep more information than you need and avoid negative comments or storing health data.

- Individuals have rights to ask for a copy of all personal information held on them. You need to be certain that if someone does, it would not reveal anything embarrassing or that breaches data protection law.

This is not intended to be legal advice and you should take specific legal advice from an experienced data law practitioner in relation to your own business circumstances and legal jurisdiction.

If you use the Propella business intelligence software you will be given further guidelines on GDPR.

Understanding the Propella quadrants and plotting some of your groups, organisations, and people on the grid is just the start. There's more to come.

Remember, Propella sits above your other marketing and communications activities, and your future focus will be on your VIPs and Upgraders.

Now we're going to look at the Propella characters.

CHAPTER EIGHT

The Characters (And Meet Your New Best Friend)

Once your plotting is complete, a character set emerges that deserves your special attention. You'll recognise all of the characters, and some will *really* resonate. Meet them first, then put names next to them and discover what action to take. Priority characters need to be converted into the VIP box and kept there. Propella is a working tool, and these priority characters change positions as your focused marketing starts to work. Some characters will need watching and some can be ignored. By the end of the next three chapters, you will know all the characters and be able to:

- Apply them to your situation(s)

- Spot them by their characteristics

- Have a game plan for each one

- Understand how your relationship looks from their point of view

Here's a speed-dating introduction with their screen icons.

The Ambassador (R>75/L>75) – Always top-right of the VIP quadrant; organisations and people who will recommend you and offer protection in a crisis.

The Assassin (R>75/L<0) – Always outside top-left quadrant; high on Royalty but *negative* on Loyalty, they are damaging your business.

The Boomerang (R>50/L 25–50) – Upgrader; usually a former client, newly lost pitch opportunity, contact, or employee who *could* be encouraged to return. The bigger the Boomerang, the closer to the top of the quadrant they are.

The Eager Beaver – Moves around on the border between No Frills and Upgrader or Standard and Upgrader; an ambitious organisation or person on the way up, with or without your help (but preferably with).

The Prize (aka the Big Daddy) (R>75/L<50) – Upgrader; a target that others will follow.

The Trojan Horse (R>50/L<50) – Upgrader; you know someone on the inside.

The Mirage (R>50/L<25) – Upgrader, sometimes disguised as the Prize; a *very* attractive-looking potential client. But, reality check needed, they will *never* choose you.

The Smiley (R<50/L>50) – Organisation or person in Standard; nice to spend time with but will never give you work or whatever else you need to succeed.

The Pirate – Competitors circling the grid to take your clients, talent, ideas, and advantage.

The Deadweight (R<25/L<25) – Always at the very bottom of No Frills; an organisation or person unimportant to you and that often takes your precious time and energy with limited upside. They weigh you down, if you let them.

Here they all are, at their starting points.

Fig 8.1 Propella with all the characters at their starting points

Before finding out more and what to do with them, meet the most important character outside and inside your business, your new best friend: the Ambassador.

The Ambassador

Ambassadors are like diamonds – precious, rare, valuable, inimitable, highly prized, hard-earned, and easily lost through carelessness. You don't need many diamonds to look brilliant. A couple of whoppers will dazzle and have massive impact!

Ambassadors are recommending your firm often without you asking them or knowing about it. Oh, and without any money exchanging hands – the dream ticket.

They are yours for life if you look after them. No matter what your business or where you are on your strategic journey, if you look after your Ambassadors, you will reap rewards and accelerate that journey.

Ambassadors are your biggest and most loyal supporters. They act as an extension of your marketing, recruitment, and reputation-management departments – in fact, your whole organisation. In a time of crisis, these people become a 'force field' around your business. Here is your relationship capital. Working closely with Ambassadors is your passport to word of mouth, the most valuable marketing tool of them all.

The more you work with your Ambassadors, the more you show them how much you value their support, the stronger the circle of trust becomes. Knowing who these people are will bring absolute focus on how best to spend your marketing time and money.

Characteristics

Setting the co-ordinates, the all-important 50 markers on your Propella grid, is the first step in identifying your Ambassadors. Ambassadors are usually visible, but you may not have noticed or appreciated them. With some reframing, focus, homework, and emotional intelligence (EQ), you will see them clearly. Here are

Fig 8.2 Propella showing Ambassador – the most important character of all.

Gladwell's Mavens, Connectors, and Salesmen.[32] Here are Everett Rogers' innovators and early adopters.[33] Here is your fan base, your inner circle.

- Externally, they are highly influential in your space. Extremely well known, they have a voice that counts. And it's a voice that recommends you. They are big-spender clients sending you their best business. They add kudos, they are reliable, they bring something extra to your events, they pay on time, they share your news, and people take notice.

- Internally, they are the people to whom everyone turns for advice, guidance, and leadership. They are the 'tribal elders' (although not necessarily old) with extensive influence. They are the trendsetters – others will often mirror what they wear, what they say, and how they behave. They might be Ambassadors for only one aspect of your business. They are loyal to you and will be keen to make an impression. They love their job and the business. If you want to speed up an internal behaviour change, it's your internal Ambassadors who will get the job done for you.

- Among your contact base, they are the exceptionally well-connected, natural networkers who regularly make introductions for you.

---

32 Gladwell, *The Tipping Point*.
33 Rogers, *Diffusion of Innovations*.

- Ambassadors are likely to have been with you for a long time. The fierce loyalty of a true Ambassador doesn't happen overnight.

- Perhaps you have done something extraordinary for them that they will never forget. You have 'touched' their life in a memorable way, and the impression you made has remained. It could be a work experience or a personal one. You may have shared some challenging and/or extraordinary times. You may have made them look good or saved them from something.

- It's highly likely you have some shared corporate or personal values.

- There is a spark, a spoken or unspoken connection, beyond the formal relationship.

- You are confident that if you called them now, they would welcome the call. You have their direct line, their mobile number, and possibly their home number. They have yours, don't they?

- They are like magnets for people seeking advice or a recommendation. Others look at them and say, 'I'll have what they're having.'

- Almost always, Ambassadors will go beyond the call of duty to help you out. Having more than one Ambassador makes it easier to share the load and not abuse any single relationship.

- Friends are different from Ambassadors, but Ambassadors may become friends.

How to spot them

A true Ambassador is often exclusive to you in your business sector. As you develop your Propella grid, you will find that you have Ambassadors for different occasions, drawn from various stakeholder types. Some names might pop into your head instantly (and you might realise you haven't contacted them for ages). Others will emerge as the Propella grid is built.

Some homework combined with EQ and asking around your organisation will reveal a few more. Quantity doesn't matter. You will have at least one. The point is to create the *right* number for your business.

Ambassadors are for life. You should find a way to value retired Ambassadors.

Your mission

Make your Ambassadors feel looked after and special at all times. This is your opportunity to create a superpower marketing, recruitment, and reputation-management department working for you 24/7.

When I was explaining this to a group of Millennials, all professionals working on how to look after their Ambassadors, they looked at me quizzically and asked, 'Do you mean they need to feel the love?' Yes, that's exactly what I mean!

Game plan

Wow these people at *every* interaction. You can deliver a highly personalised communications programme at the level required to only a small number of people. These are those people.

Be one step ahead of what they're doing. Remove them from commoditised marketing tools as much as possible. Follow all the rules for how to treat VIPs and then add some.

Ambassadors should have everything first. They often return your courtesy by giving you things first. Early notice of potential work. Industry information. A heads-up on someone joining or leaving. First call on a new contract.

They are your circle of trust, so consult with them from time to time. Their objectivity will provide an invaluable 360-degree view.

Build a small Ambassadors 'board' – a sounding board – to give you early feedback on ideas or initiatives. True Ambassadors give feedback with pleasure because they value the association. You might build Ambassador 'clusters' with a common denominator, e.g. sector, client type, service line, gender, location. Use different Ambassadors for different occasions and play to their strengths. Remember the earlier point about the credentials of the messenger? An Upgrader, say the Prize or Boomerang, is more likely to listen to someone like them. Having a selection of Ambassador 'types' means you can match the right Ambassador to the right Upgrader. For example, if you're targeting over-40 female entrepreneurs, choose an Ambassador with the same credentials.

Ambassadors should be receiving your best marketing, be speaking at your events, appearing in videos on your website, and acting as your referees. Identify *potential* Ambassadors and create as many as you can reasonably manage. Once you have too many, share the management of them.

As you progress through *The Power of Personal*, you'll realise how much you're going to rely on this group of people.

Here's a useful test. Think about organisations for whom you are an Ambassador and ask yourself how you like to be treated. Something as simple as someone knowing your name when you call is appreciated. We all know how good it feels when someone recognises us, is pleased to hear from us, and remembers something about the last interaction we had with them. Ask yourself how you would like this organisation to communicate with you.

Ambassadors should not be confused with the following:

- Brand ambassadors, who might be 'celebrities' paid for brand association. While these people have purpose in B2C, they are irrelevant here. Propella Ambassadors don't expect payment, and that's the point. They are pleased to recommend you.

- Brand advocates, who are more relevant for brands relying on social media approval. For an excellent overview of brand advocates, I recommend Rob Fuggetta's book *Brand Advocates – Turning Enthusiastic Customers into a Powerful Marketing Force*.[34] Brand advocates in this largely consumer marketing context are so numerous that it would be challenging to filter them, let alone *know* them. Social media profile is one of several criteria to take into account on the Royalty axis.

- Influencers, especially third parties, those being paid to influence, or serial influencers. Some

34 R. Fuggetta, *Brand Advocates – Turning Enthusiastic Customers into a Powerful Marketing Force* (Hoboken, NJ: John Wiley & Sons, 2012).

153

Propella Ambassadors may *also* be influencers but aren't asked or paid to recommend you. They are already out there doing it. Propella is not about 'influencer' marketing.

Health warning

Looking after Ambassadors takes time but not necessarily money. However, I cannot tell you how rewarding and even enjoyable this is – you have to try it yourself. The benefits heavily outweigh the effort involved. Within reason, a real Ambassador won't mind being asked for help, but don't overload or abuse the relationship. The smart move is to create an army of Ambassadors and call on them individually, depending on the challenge.

How your relationship looks to them

Fantastic. You treat them as individuals. They feel special and important to you.

Bonus thought

What are the qualities of the Ambassador? If you have an affinity with a certain type of Ambassador, it's likely you will appeal to those with similar characteristics in the Upgrader quadrant.

Boutique pensions practice Pension Partners provides a 'white label' pension team to law firms without their own pensions capability. Using the Propella grid, Pension Partners quickly established the qualities of their Ambassador law firms and people so they could repeat their success with other law firms.

Kate Ive, founding partner of Pension Partners:

'We quickly saw that our best law firm clients shared certain qualities, including high-quality corporate and employment teams, ambitious growth plans and a positive attitude to innovative working. We selected our other target law firms based on those qualities and positioned our offer to them exclusively. As a result, we now act for a number of law firms providing a seamless pension service to their clients.'

Coming up next: the characters you need to convert.

CHAPTER NINE

Characters To Convert

Now that you have your Ambassadors, turn your attention to the promising Upgrader characters – the Prize, the Trojan Horse, and the Boomerang. These characters have the *potential* to become VIPs and Ambassadors, so your marketing and communications need to move them across that 50 marker on the Loyalty axis. We'll also look at how to convert the Assassin (see Fig 9.1).

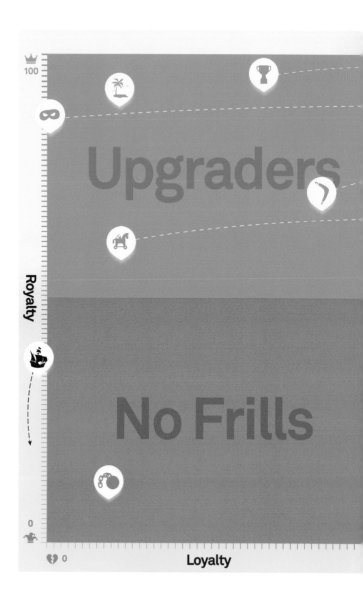

Fig 9.1 Propella showing character conversions

The Prize

Converting this character is immensely satisfying and excellent for business.

Characteristics

The Prize is an organisation or person with the potential to become a 'trophy' client that others follow (aka a lighthouse[35] client). Converting this character into a

---

35   E. Rogers, *Diffusion of Innovations*.

VIP and onwards to an Ambassador can be a game changer. The Prize may be one of the following:

- A significant organisation in the sector you want to be famous in. Others will think, 'If they're good enough for [the Prize], then they must be good.' Their endorsement spreads horizontally and vertically.

- A potential employee from a competitor who will bring other people, clients, and status.

- The biggest title or blogger on your media list. Once they mention you, others will take you seriously.

- An employee who will influence others.

- An organisation you want to partner with but that appears out of reach.

- A productive high-profile contact who has an established relationship with a competitor and whose endorsement could make a transformative difference.

The signs will be obvious. You'll 'just know' your Prizes the second you place them on the grid.

Not to be confused with the unrealistic Mirage. With a Prize, there is a sense of possibility.

Fig 9.2 Propella showing Prize

Sometimes can be converted to the Trojan Horse. It's always thrilling to find you know someone on the inside.

How to spot them

You look at them longingly. They look slightly out of reach. The very thought of working with them is both exciting and slightly scary. In your business plan, even the one in your head, they are aspirational. In your dreams, they are walking into your office ready to shake hands and be shown around. Winning them is a stretch, but a realistic stretch.

Your mission

Win them.

Game plan

Make them a priority. Assign your best team to them, and put yourself in charge of that team. Activate your internal and external Ambassadors. Prizes must be earned.

Health warning

Prepare for the long haul. Gird your loins for rejection. And don't miss a beat.

How your relationship looks to them

Some risk and a leap of faith are required on their part. They will need to cross a trust line to be confident you can deliver. They need reassurance on brand, hierarchy, and values alignment. Something in your offer might resonate with them, and they'll go with that. They may test you with a small, low-risk piece of business (although to you, it will be big and momentous).

Bonus thought

When a Prize is won, you a) celebrate b) tell the world (with their permission) c) start the programme to create a new Ambassador.

Law firm A had an automotive-sector group with a 'world domination' mission. Clients included small-to-medium-sized companies in the automotive sector. With the right combination of genuine expertise, profile, leadership, and commitment, they eventually won a small piece of work for the national office of a global manufacturer. The firm invested heavily in wowing this client and continued to impress them with outstanding work and client service. They gradually built up the volume and range of work until the manufacturer appointed them to its panel. Firm A used that name to attract other automotive clients.

The Trojan Horse

The Trojan Horse is a rare beast, but discovering one on your grid is the best kind of surprise, and a terrific bonus.

Characteristics

The Trojan Horse is an Upgrader organisation where you know someone on the inside. You recognise their face in that company's press coverage or spot their name in an organisation chart and your heart skips a beat. You hear yourself saying, 'I know that person!' Seeking information on Upgraders from people within your business is recommended (remember, Propella is a team game) because you extend the possibility of discovering a Trojan Horse. The closer to the top of the Upgrader quadrant, the bigger the Trojan Horse. Sometimes that insider might be why you chose the target. Some Trojan Horses emerge after the target has been chosen.

The perfect storm is a Trojan Horse/Prize combination. I've seen people laugh out loud when this happens.

Or, smart move, create a Trojan Horse by placing one of your own on the inside as a secondee.

Fig 9.3 Propella showing Trojan Horse

Accountancy firm (AF) advises directors of major corporate (MC) on personal tax issues. Keen to expand their portfolio with MC, AF hears from a director that MC is urgently looking for international tax talent on a strategic project. AF's offer of star-performer junior partner for six months is accepted immediately. The junior partner reports back on what's happening in MC (without breaching any confidentiality restrictions) while talking up AF and looking for opportunities to pitch other service offerings. Within twelve months, AF is given the opportunity to pitch for an expanded portfolio.

How to spot them

It's easy to check what contacts you have *within* a business, starting with LinkedIn company pages. You can also look at their websites and run through all the people to see who you might know. Read the people profiles to work out who does what and their seniority. Organisation charts are sometimes buried in websites if you know where to look. Be open to asking people in your own firm if they know anybody in that organisation. This approach often delivers surprising results – your colleagues and employees might just know a pivotal person through another workplace, their education/training, or a sports club. On one occasion, a Trojan Horse was a colleague's spouse! Other common Trojan Horses are your own alumni and people who moved from your clients and contacts into this organisation but a) weren't, at the time, senior enough for you to notice (see the health warning in

Eager Beaver), or b) their move wasn't tracked. I've seen people discover long-lost peer-group contacts from school, university, or college. These are slightly more challenging to pursue, but there's nothing to lose. Worst-case scenario… the Trojan Horse is an old flame. In this case, change the target!

The test: If you or one of your colleagues called this person out of the blue, would they know your name or that of the person calling? Would they take the call? And if so, would they feel positive about it? If yes, then it's game on.

Your mission

Convert this person into a highly valuable Ambassador. Get in touch with them by email or via LinkedIn at first. The early reconnection requires diplomacy. This may take time, but less time than it will take to convert a normal Upgrader.

Game plan

Go carefully and woo them as you would any Upgrader. Arrange a one-to-one short meeting, perhaps over coffee, at a time and place convenient for that person. Clarify the agenda before you meet. You are asking for help. Give them space to decline rather than catch them unaware. Also, be very careful not to incite any revealing of confidential information. Never offer a financial or reward incentive – this is completely inappropriate and runs the risk of contravening bribery legislation or company policy. The range of help offered could include anything from an overview of the key people to an honest opinion about your chances of winning any work, insight on competitor performance, a download of current opportunities, and full-blown introductions to the right people. Take what's on offer and don't push it. Maintain contact with that person after the ball gets rolling. You must respect their position. People should never feel used. Also think about what you can do to return the favour. It might be a favour that's paid forward or notched up for use later, so listen carefully.

Treat people as you would like to be treated. You might be someone else's Trojan Horse. If that someone contacted you out of the blue asking for similar help, would you respond positively? If yes, then good karma is on its way.

Health warning

The colder the contact, the harder it is to make the conversion. Again, you should never use people or be perceived to be using them. While making connections and asking for introductions is accepted as enterprising practice, sometimes it isn't appropriate. Think about what's in it for them before you make the approach. If you have any doubt, don't do it. A Trojan Horse only works when it feels right. While it's always good to know someone in an Upgrader business, this person needs to be a senior someone rather than a junior someone. I had a client whose Upgrader list contained the senior management teams of ten London law firms. A former trainee was a junior lawyer in one of these firms – unfortunately, this person didn't qualify as a Trojan Horse because they had no *current* influence on the senior management team (but could be a long-term investment – see Eager Beaver).

Be very careful when approaching friends, neighbours, or family members. Don't abuse a personal relationship to win business.

How to increase your chances of finding them

- Two degrees of separation means you can improve your chances of finding Trojan Horses by building a large LinkedIn network. Build your network *before* you need it. Encourage your team to do the same and make it easy for them to post your organisation's news on LinkedIn so that their networks, which may include a future Trojan Horse, are already somewhere on the Propella grid's Recognition, Reputation, Recommendation journey.

- Ensure your alumni programme keeps track of former employees.

- Track people moving jobs. Once you're tuned in to these moves, more names will emerge. Connecting with them on LinkedIn and checking notifications means you're always on top of their career moves. Many times, I've seen a client's contact move into an Upgrader organisation.

- Attend relevant networking events and sector conferences with the aim of finding or creating a Trojan Horse.

- Be aware of where your friends and neighbours work and the people they know. I don't mean in a secret police kind of way. I mean just be aware. There is a balance to be achieved here.

How your relationship looks to them

Surprising, initially. But most people respond posi-tively to requests for help and will be honest about what they can or can't do. At the very least, they may direct you to the right person.

The Boomerang

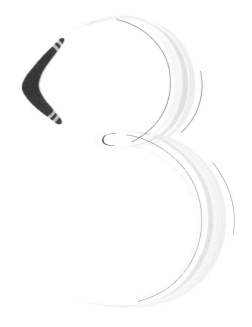

Here's an interesting, oft-neglected character.

Characteristics

A Boomerang is usually a former client who could be encouraged to return. It could be a client who feels they have outgrown you, a client who feels neglected, or a client who wants to pay less (say under some pressure

175

Fig 9.4 Propella showing Boomerang

from the procurement professionals). A newly created Boomerang is the target client where you came a close second on the pitch. A contact Boomerang used to give you their best referrals but has now gone silent. Or the Boomerang could be a star employee who was wooed by a competitor with a big golden hello and you want them back.

The bigger the Boomerang, the closer to the top of the Upgrader quadrant they are. The thing about Boomerangs is they must be *worth* having back.

Not to be confused with someone who is playing you off against a competitor for, say, a cost gain. They are not worth working with.

How to spot them

It's easy. They used to be on your client list, top of your referral register, and at your parties. Now they're not. You miss them.

Your mission

Win them back. Start now because the longer it's left, the tougher it is. After a year, Boomerangs revert to normal Upgraders but are further away than ever.

Game plan

Treat them like your best VIPs and Upgraders – wow them and woo them, even though they're working with a competitor. Choose the best person to do the wooing. Call on your Ambassadors for help, especially those still loyal to you in the Boomerang organisation. This is a confident move, and those Boomerangs won't be expecting it. Neither will the competitor who took them. Be patient. Your time will come. Monitor the competitor because sooner or later, they will reveal a weakness that presents the opportunity to strike with a competitive advantage.

Health warning

It might take time, but with carefully executed communications, it's totally possible to win Boomerangs back.

How your relationship looks to them

Risky. They left your firm for a reason. They won't make the same mistake twice. You must address why they left and reassure them about what's changed. Note that the exit or handover interview, or pitch debrief, is when the work starts on winning them back.

How to avoid creating them in the first place

Follow the advice on how to look after your VIPs to pick up any contentious issues early on. Look for signs of new people being appointed to decision-making roles, replacing your contacts, and diverting loyalty to competitors. For clients and employees, you may also be fortunate enough to spot the early warning signs of a move and can mitigate the fall-out. A tell-tale sign is knowledgeable referencing of competitor information, especially anything relating to money. Once you're using Propella to its fullest potential, the risk of losing a client is minimised.

Long-standing client told their medium-sized regional accountancy firm that they wanted bigger advisers. Client felt they had outgrown the firm. They wanted broader service lines and the status of working with a Big Four accountant. Rather than resist, the firm's managing partner took a lead role on the recruitment and appointment process, oversaw an efficient and friendly handover, and maintained contact. She then waited. Within twelve months, the client, unimpressed by the anonymity of Big Four people, being billed for every second, and feeling distinctly unimportant, returned to the original firm. They all lived happily ever after!

The Assassin

Characteristics

The Assassin is a person right up the top of the Royalty axis but negative on the Loyalty axis. These individuals may, possibly intentionally, destroy your reputation and damage your business. Occasionally, it can extend to an organisation where many people become poisoned from the inside by the Assassin. Triggers for creating Assassins are many and various. Propella Assassins – and this is crucial – have *always* been created by the organisation they are damaging and the window of opportunity for an early apology has passed. They must be swiftly converted to minimise the ongoing damage.

181

Fig 9.5 Propella showing Assassin (the worse they are, the more they are to the left)

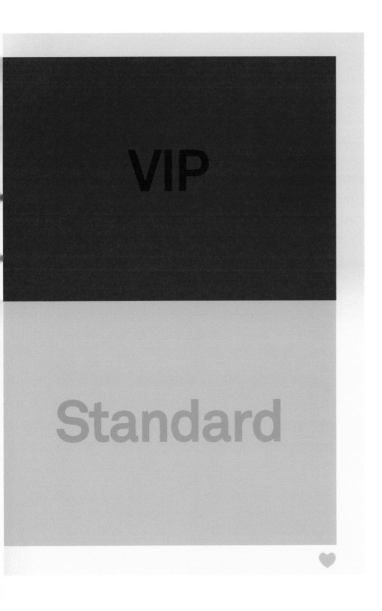

Common Assassins:

- A journalist or blogger who persistently negatively references a person or firm. This Assassin might feel slighted by something surprisingly trivial and unintended. I knew one who went on the offensive with a whole firm because the senior partner cancelled a lunch at short notice. By short, I mean that the journalist in question was waiting in the restaurant. A cast-iron way to create a media Assassin is to tell them a lie – you will be found out.

- An internal Assassin who feels mistreated and leaks confidential inside information (note, not a whistleblower who is uncovering a serious internal wrong).

- A former disgruntled employee who left in challenging circumstances and is now working for a client or a competitor.

Firm A underwent a difficult redundancy programme. People were asked to leave on performance grounds even though there had been no prior indication of performance issues. Although the redundancy terms were generous, the execution of the departure for these individuals was embarrassing. They were forbidden to say goodbye to colleagues or plan an orderly exit. Within weeks, one redundancy candidate turned up in a VIP client organisation and wreaked havoc.

- A dissatisfied former client whose influence was underestimated and who wasn't properly 'dealt with' on exit. They're now sharing their bad experience with everyone they meet.

With all Assassins, sometimes the true cost of the original disagreement is far greater than its financial value.

Not to be confused with people who are guilty of libelling or slandering you or your business. These are for a specialist lawyer to deal with.

How to spot them

There are two types: noisy and quiet. The noisy ones are relatively easy to tackle because they're in your line of sight. The most dangerous of those are active on social media and their blurring of lines between truth and fiction goes unchecked.

Social media didn't exist when Sir Winston Churchill said, 'A lie gets halfway around the world before the truth has a chance to get its pants on.' Imagine how fast lies get around now.

The quiet Assassins, usually internal, *appear* to be on your side but, in reality, are not. Look for passive-aggressive behaviour. More active ones dish out poison, spread gossip and negative messages. Left unchecked they do untold damage.

185

I'm always amazed by how many clients admit to having Assassins they (metaphorically) brush under the carpet. They avoid dealing with them despite how severely they can limit their progress.

Your mission

Neutralise their attitude towards you. A long haul, but possible, is to convert them into Ambassadors.

Game plan

Call on the wisdom and status of your Ambassadors to neutralise the attitude of your Assassin. With enough Ambassadors (remember my advice to create Ambassador clusters), you can match the Ambassador according to the Assassin. If the situation has tipped into crisis management, this is when your Ambassadors can become a 'force field' around your business.

- A senior person from the business or your best client or contact Ambassador (individually or combined) could neutralise the negative journalist's attitude – someone whose opinion that journalist values or finds useful. That's the starting point to a relationship turnaround.

- A disgruntled former employee should be neutralised by someone they respect in a face-to-face meeting that starts with a big apology. Often, the disgruntled employee just wants to be heard. Treat these meetings as a learning experience to avoid a repeat occurrence.

- The most senior person in the organisation needs to meet with the dissatisfied former client, listen to their views, and reach a compromise.

Barrister chambers A was working hard on growing market share in a highly competitive niche market. Constantly talking them down in that market was a QC in rival chambers B whose tenancy application for A was once-upon-a-time-in-the-dim-and-distant-past declined. Head of A, also a QC, was sent on a peace mission. The rival QC was flattered by the attention of A's QC and felt his point had been made. It was never a best-friends scenario, but the talking down stopped.

Health warning

Deal with Propella Assassins early – the longer the time between the original affront and the correction attempt, the less likely the chance of putting things right. Avoid creating clusters of Assassins with shared interests. In line with common sense, defamation laws, and GDPR, do not say or record anything defamatory about this person on any database or otherwise.

Sally Mewies, Technology and Data partner at Gowling WLG:

> 'If that person were, for example, to make a subject access request, which they are entitled to do under GDPR, you risk having to disclose information that could jeopardise the chances of an improved relationship making an unsatisfactory situation even worse.'

Remember, a Propella Assassin is one you have unintentionally created.

How your relationship looks to them

Assassins want your attention and they will keep going unless you stop them. Most Assassins respond positively to the reconciliation efforts because you have given them what they wanted.

How to avoid creating them in the first place

Conduct client-service and exit interviews. Listen to your clients and deal with their complaints. To avoid creating Assassins out of employees, consider exit interviews, including at redundancy and retirement. Use integrity to deal with both. Have the difficult conversations or the Assassins will have them, on repeat, with others at your considerable expense. Ultimately it's about treating people with respect, even when the pressure is on. For the media, there is good media relations practice and taking the advice of a public relations professional. Media Assassins are often created because public relations professionals were not involved in the first place.

In all cases, an early and authentic apology from the right person can mitigate the creation of an Assassin.

We've dealt with the characters to convert. Coming next are the ones to watch.

CHAPTER TEN

Characters To Watch

You now know the characters most worthy of your time and attention. Your Ambassadors are your number one priority. Wow them, day in, day out. Next on the list are those with conversion potential – ultimately, your future Ambassadors – the Prize, the Trojan Horse, and the Boomerang. And finally, there are the Assassins, who need converting for different reasons.

The next three cohorts need to be *watched*. If allowed, one may rob you of precious time and attention that should be lavished on Ambassadors, Prizes, etc. They could easily divert you from your goal: introducing the Mirage. Two need to be watched because they're potentially more valuable than you think: introducing the Eager Beaver and the Pirate.

The Mirage

The Mirage is an all-consuming character best acknowledged and dealt with.

Characteristics

This organisation or person sits close to the top of the Upgrader quadrant, sometimes disguised as the Prize. The Mirage looks highly desirable and very attainable. It isn't. No matter what you do, it's *never* coming your way. A Mirage is almost always a target client, contact, partner, or employee. Here are some common characteristics of Mirages, but note that the Mirage has many disguises and this is not an exhaustive list.

- They are *forever* loyal to one of your competitors. That loyalty is driven by history, personal relationships, long-standing associations that have become friendships, or a combination of these things. The reasons might seem unfathomable to you. Sometimes people are loyal to a particular person no matter where they work. Your Mirage is a competitor's Ambassador.

- Because of your size or brand differences, they perceive you as too small or inappropriate for them. A Mirage will gladly take your hospitality but never return the favour.

- They might seem like an obvious match and you may have been given what you perceive to be encouraging signs, but there are controlling factors elsewhere; perhaps there is an influential person behind the scenes who had a negative experience with your firm.

- They may invite you to pitch or attend an interview because they want to negotiate terms with their existing firm. They may want some free advice or to 'extract' useful insights and ideas they know you'll give away in your enthusiasm. A badly behaved Mirage might do this on behalf of a competitor. It could be a box-ticking exercise. They give you hope, and you respond, with your A team, by being generous and helpful. Having whetted your appetite and got what they wanted, they disappear without trace.

Fig 10.1 Propella showing Mirage

- The relationship is one-way.

- A common sign is a lack of manners – they don't say thank you, or they show up late or not at all without an apology. You are forgiving, of course, because you *think* you're dealing with a Prize. You're not. It's a Mirage.

You may be lucky and never experience a Mirage. Thankfully, it's a rare beast, but hugely dangerous when it appears. The hardest thing about a Mirage is that you don't want to believe it's a Mirage.

My first experience with a Mirage was in an accountancy firm. Out of the blue, the firm was sent an invitation to tender (ITT) from a major public service department based in the same region. The firm was flattered that the public service department had put them on the tender list, even though this department had previously been regarded as unattainable *and* undesirable. Now the ITT had landed, previous opinions were discarded. What this firm refused to see was that it was on a list of twenty local organisations asked to pitch as a token gesture to the regional business community.

The whole pitch process was designed to challenge the existing advisers on fees and service levels. But, never mind the facts – a Mirage can make you behave oddly. Delusions are common. This firm went all out to win the work. There were special meeting rooms, all-night meetings, teams of top people siphoned away from fee-earning to focus on this proposal, designers commissioned to produce the report, novelty ideas introduced to impress and dazzle, a video commissioned to introduce the team, researchers commissioned to deep dive the sector, business development people pulled in to work exclusively on this proposal, and consultants brought in to spot anything missing.

Well, you know how the story ends. They didn't make it past first base, and they never would have. The work went back to the incumbents.

The disappointment was palpable. Those involved felt crushed. And more realistic opportunities had been overlooked in the time spent on the proposal.

I've seen versions of this scenario played out many times since, and always with the same result.

Your mission

Be brave. Leave the Mirage alone and concentrate on the real Prizes. Feel free to keep sending them marketing information if it makes *you* feel good, but accept that it's not going to happen, unless circumstances change.

Game plan

Resist temptation.

Health warning

A Mirage can make you temporarily lose your senses.

How your relationship looks to them

It's not a relationship. You are the means to a pre-defined end.

How to avoid them in the first place

Ask them directly about their true intentions. The truth might hurt, but it saves time and misguided effort. A Mirage will respect you more for asking. Or, do thorough research and be honest with yourself – you may not be ready for this organisation. Note that a Mirage may reveal their true agenda to a third party.

The director of a rapidly growing family-owned business (FB) with significant spend was being hotly pursued by accountancy firm A, who was keen to displace long-standing, smaller accountancy firm B. This business looked like a Prize. It was high on firm A's target list, and they were investing heavily in winning them to the detriment of pursuing more realistic targets. An FB director shared with a third party that although they had outgrown firm B, they would never move to another supplier. Firm B had once helped them in a tricky family situation and saved them tens of thousands of pounds and considerable embarrassment.

The Eager Beaver

The Eager Beaver is a much-admired and popular character who could repay your loyalty many times over in the right circumstances.

Characteristics

Ambition is the distinctive trait of this organisation or person heading only upwards. Eager Beavers float (but not for long because they move quickly) on the borders between No Frills and Upgrader or the point between Standard and Upgrader. The real-deal Eager Beaver has *masses* of potential and talent but might be

199

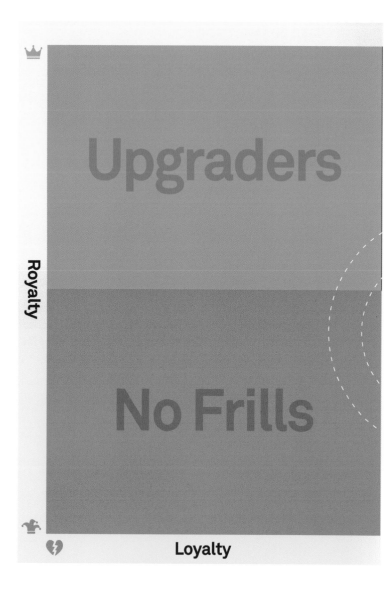

Fig 10.2 Propella showing Eager Beaver, a character that, to start with, quickly moves around in this radar

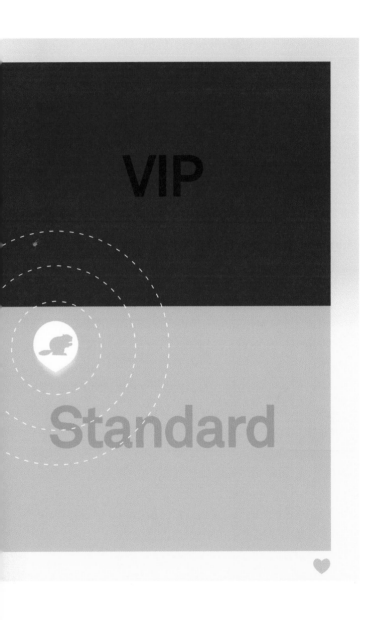

underestimated and overlooked as too junior or insignificant. Huge mistake.

Common Eager Beavers:

- A business new to your client sector, probably disruptive, challenging the status quo.

- A newly appointed junior person in a client, contact, or media team.

- An employee in your own organisation keen for promotion.

Eager Beavers often appear from nowhere. Whatever or whoever they are, Eager Beavers are worth watching because they invariably end up Upgraders with value, influence, and power. If you spot the signs and help them, you create an overnight VIP or, better still, an Ambassador.

How to spot them

Noisy ones will let *you* know they exist. They make themselves heard in the media, especially social media, and volunteer for useful roles – anywhere they will be noticed. Eager Beavers can be challenging but bring a welcome energy. Run with that energy.

The quiet, unassuming ones operating just below the radar can be elusive. They may give you one chance to notice them. You see their names on reports. They ask you questions (sometimes those that others are afraid to ask but always in your best interests). They want a teensy-weensy bit of help. They ask for small favours. They are givers not takers, radiators not drainers. They're looking at you. They want to be in your tribe. They want to connect with you on social media. Sometimes they might appear as the underdog, not a status they occupy for very long.

They might circle outside a meeting, being useful and waiting for the chance to be given bigger responsibilities. If someone on your team is unexpectedly absent, you can be sure the Eager Beaver will step in, hoover it up, and shine. Eager Beavers have long memories and remember those who helped them on the way up. And who didn't. Real Eager Beavers are smart and will move elsewhere if they don't get what they want. Sooner or later, you'll see them again.

Your mission

Invest a little time and effort in them for the potential reward of creating a future Ambassador.

Game plan

Notice them, remember them, acknowledge them, and give them access to the circle of trust. The Eager Beaver really appreciates small kindnesses: advice, guidance, a conversation, a good reference, association, praise (especially in front of others), thanks, respect. Looking after them is a doddle. They want very little, just to feel included and noticed. You will reap rich rewards if you make them feel this way.

Health warning

Eager Beavers are for life. Real beavers, as it happens, are monogamous. Look out for Eager Beavers joining a VIP or Upgrader. You'll be so very glad you looked after them. An Eager Beaver makes the best Ambassador.

How your relationship looks to them

As if everything is possible and it's only a matter of time. It's personal for the Eager Beaver.

Here are my favourite examples of high-profile Eager Beavers.

In 1976, Meryl Streep was told she was 'too ugly' to star in *King Kong*. Fast-forward to 2015; she recalled that feedback and shared it with millions of people while collecting one of her eighteen Academy Awards:

'This was a pivotal moment for me. This one rogue opinion could derail my dreams of becoming an actress or force me to pull myself up by the boot straps and believe in myself.

'I took a deep breath and said, "I'm sorry you think I'm too ugly for your film but you're just one opinion in a sea of thousands and I'm off to find a kinder tide".[36]

J. K. Rowling received many rejections before finding a publisher for what became the Harry Potter series. Her agent, Christopher Little, later recalled that he wrote back to her within four days of receiving the manuscript: 'I thought there was something really special there, although we could never have guessed what would happen to it.'[37] He sold it to Bloomsbury and later reaped huge rewards from international rights.

It pays to spot an Eager Beaver.

More recently, Rowling received further rejections, for her first adult fiction manuscripts written under a pseudonym. She later revealed the names of the publishers who rejected her.[38]

It pays not to mess with an Eager Beaver.

Eager Beaver organisations and people like Meryl Streep and J. K. Rowling are in your circle of influence right now.

36 Harriet Alexander, 'Meryl Streep told she was "too ugly" to act in King Kong', *The Telegraph*, 11 November 2015. https://www.telegraph.co.uk/news/worldnews/northamerica/usa/11988870/Meryl-Streep-told-she-was-too-ugly-to-act-in-King-Kong.html.

37 David Smith, 'Harry Potter and the man who conjured up Rowling's millions', *The Guardian*, 15 July 2007. https://www.theguardian.com/business/2007/jul/15/harrypotter.books.

38 Hannah Furness, 'JK Rowling reveals cringe-worthy rejection letter telling her to join writing class', *The Telegraph*, 25 March 2016. http://www.telegraph.co.uk/books/news/jk-rowling-reveals-cringe-worthy-rejection-letter-telling-her-to/.

The Pirate

Pirates are your competitors. They circle your grid looking for what can be taken. Though immensely irritating, they are oh-so useful if you watch them carefully.

Characteristics

Above or below you in your peer group, competitors and their people are constantly after your VIP clients, people, contacts, and suppliers. If they take them, they'll celebrate. Pirates are a fact of life. I have seen clients obsessed with, even driven to distraction, by competitors. I prefer to think of Propella Pirates as fun Pirates. There is a game to be played and to win this game, you need to outwit Pirates and be one step ahead.

Not to be confused with an Assassin. A Pirate will not wilfully damage your business, as an Assassin will. Pirates are in the same game, and it's played out in the open.

How to spot them

It's easy. You share the same market and stakeholders. You have a healthy respect for each other. But their success bothers you. Look out for challenger brands and disruptors – they often have compelling offers and move quickly.

Your mission

Take Michael Corleone's advice: 'Keep your friends close, but your enemies closer.'[39]

Game plan

Pirate activity can be strangely stimulating. Pirates stop you becoming complacent.

---

39 *The Godfather Part II* (Paramount Pictures, 1974, directed by Francis Ford Coppola).

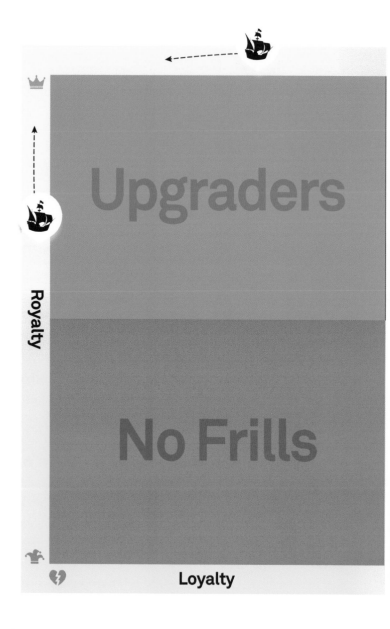

Fig 10.3 Propella with circling Pirates

Monitor them, learn from them, and use their weaknesses to leverage *your* competitive advantage to take *their* clients, people, and contacts. But play fair. One day they will reveal a weakness that opens up an opportunity for you. Say, if a key person leaves a competitor, this is the time to look at who you might want from *their* client base. Sometimes you can make deals with Pirates. For example, if a firm is conflicted-out of a particular piece of work, there are often 'conflict' arrangements in place between firms that allow work to be passed to a rival on a reciprocity basis. Look at who they are recruiting. Where are they expanding? What are they saying about themselves? How are they marketing? Where are the opportunities for you? What are they claiming for themselves that you can do better? Never rubbish them and you always maintain the moral high ground. Never copy them. Always be confident and charming, the consummate professional, when face-to-face with them. Make sure your team members know who the Pirates are. This way, they can pick up snippets of valuable information that will feed your marketing intelligence. Never let Pirates know you're bothered by them. Keep them in perspective.

Health warning

Pirates can become merger or referral partners. Joining forces with a Pirate means you can overtake a shared rival. Never do anything to a Pirate that you wouldn't like done to you. No slandering or libellous behaviour needed here. One managing partner I worked with had the healthy attitude to refer to his firm as 'the best of the best' in relation to competitors. Take the lead in the relationship, set the game rules, and ensure your people know the same. Showing respect for the competition is good for the sector.

How your relationship looks to them

Exactly as it does to you. But hopefully their obsession with you absorbs more of their energy and time.

Now, our final two characters, destined for the relegation zone.

CHAPTER ELEVEN

Characters To Relegate

The Smiley and the Deadweight are low, low, low priority.

The Smiley

The Smiley is a popular character that makes you feel good but is unlikely to contribute to your success.

Characteristics

The Smiley tends to move around in the Standard quadrant but never cross the Royalty 50 line. They recommend you but aren't powerful or connected enough to make a difference. You are more important to the Smiley than they are to you, which is a shame because they're great to spend time with and they always make you happy.

Common Smileys:

- Someone who was once a VIP or Ambassador

- A former colleague, employee, or schoolmate

- A retired client, or one heading in that direction

- A contact further down the hierarchy in their respective sector or organisation

- A smaller client for whom association with you is important

- A supplier keen to woo you

- Someone with whom you have shared good times but have outgrown

Not to be confused with the Eager Beaver, who is on their way up.

The Smiley character was inspired by a client who had no time for 'marketing' but who once a year, every year, spent two days in the company of a 'potential' work referrer at a boozy horse-racing extravaganza. Best two days of the year, according to the client! But this work referrer didn't have cases that were relevant to this client and, unless there was a transformation in the business model, never would. However, the enjoyment outweighed the value of the time.

How to spot them

They contact you more than you contact them. They'll be regulars at your events and invite you to the best places for lunch (and book the next session while you're enjoying your pudding). You're invited to their best events and they show you off to colleagues and friends. Despite their low Royalty, the Smiley doesn't irritate you. On the contrary, you're always happy to see or hear from them.

Your mission

Don't have too many of them. Balance your time out so your best effort remains invested in Ambassadors, Prizes, Trojan Horses, and Boomerangs.

Fig 11.1 Propella showing Smiley

Game plan

Give yourself permission to spend time with the Smileys. We all need Smiley people in our lives, and sometimes it's about giving more than taking. Help them where you can, introduce them to others, make them happy.

Health warnings

1. The line between business relationship and friendship can sometimes be blurred. I believe the line is crossed when people you meet in a work context come to your home for a meal. Then they become friends. Smileys are not friends in this sense, but they are friendly.

2. There are Smileys and there are Smileys. Some Smileys bring value unrelated to sales or recruitment or your big goal. They might, for example, contribute to your corporate-responsibility values.

3. Don't take advantage of their goodwill because it suits you. That's just not right on any level.

4. Check who they know before making a final decision on how to work with them in future.

How your relationship looks to them

The association with you makes them look good and is useful.

The Deadweight

The Deadweight is an organisation or person seriously unimportant to *you*, always parked at the very bottom left of the No Frills quadrant, taking your time and energy even though they aren't valuable to your business. They're rare, but when they appear, they're inevitably draining. I mention them here because when I do come across them, I'm astonished at the misplaced power and importance given to them by clients, often at a huge time cost.

Fig 11.2 Propella showing Deadweight

Characteristics

Distracting from your focus, Deadweights are organisations and people who weigh heavy on your time and resources with no chance of a return. A seasoned one will suck the life out of you the moment you walk in the room.

Sometimes mistaken for the Assassin or even the Mirage.

How to spot them

They might be one of the following:

Common Deadweights:

- A client long past their sell-by date and not part of your future

- A client with whom your association is seen as negative by others

- A client who pushes back on fees, is slow to pay, or never pays

- A contact who rocks up at every event, drinks your drinks, behaves badly, hoovers up the buffet table, monopolises your guests, and leaves

A Barristers Chambers keen to grow its clinical negligence practice was chasing a firm who once had a top reputation in this space. But they hadn't noticed that the retirement of a senior partner and an almost instant move of its clinical negligence team had decimated this firm. It was the credit controller who saved the day by pointing out that this firm owed them a substantial amount of money, some of it dating back years. The firm subsequently went into administration.

How your relationship looks to them

They have the delusion of power and importance which you actually give them by paying attention.

Your mission

Put them in perspective and so reduce their perceived power.

Game plan

Do not invest any time or effort in them.

The characters – GDPR and defamation

Propella is a business intelligence software tool designed to improve how organisations interact with their stakeholders. All stakeholders should notice a difference when you start using Propella, but the priority stakeholders will find themselves on the pleasant receiving end of much more focused communication and attention. Propella is not a depository for defamatory statements or information that might fall foul of GDPR, which covers Europe, or the equivalent current or future legislation in your country. Remember:

- The Deadweight and the Smiley may not be important to you but are not unimportant in their own right. Fine line.

- The Propella Assassin is not a bad person. This is a character you may well have created yourself, and it may be wise to make amends.

People are entitled to request that you provide them with any information you keep on them. Please use Propella wisely.

In this section, you were introduced to the Propella methodology and characters. You're probably already thinking about how your own clients and targets fit in.

Next, we'll look at personalisation – how you can introduce a new level of marketing communications for your priorities and accelerate the progress of your plans.

SECTION 4
PERSONALISE – WHERE THE MAGIC HAPPENS

(Get ready to re-humanise your communications.)

CHAPTER TWELVE

Think Big

The Power of Personal started with why personalisation matters now. In Section Two, we covered what *should* be in place to connect, convince, and create exceptional client relationships. In Section Three, we looked at the Propella grid to identify the priority groups, organisations, and people who will deliver your success. You've got a communications approach for those priorities and some characters deserving your special attention. Now, the magic happens. We'll dive into the personalisation that will wow your VIPs, woo your Upgraders, activate your Ambassadors, and win your Prizes, by exploring:

- 'Know my business' = commercial closeness

- Listen big

- Be useful (no, be completely and utterly indispensable)

- Nail the opportunities closer to home

- Know my country, know my culture

This intense level of personalisation can only apply to a relatively small number of people at any one time, but the invested effort will be worth it. Those exquisite engagement moments will come thick and fast. You should look forward to making significant progress and converting characters on your Propella grid.

This *seems* like hard work at the beginning, and requires a mindset change. You may need to set aside time in your diary. Start small with a few organisations and people you can realistically manage. How many is up to you, your circumstances, your business, and the scale of your ambition – it might be just one, and that's fine. You're still building your Propella portfolio. Once you've mastered the approach, you can encourage others in your business to follow.

Empathy is completely and utterly everything here. P2P means that all marketing communications to chosen organisations and people will be personalised and tailored to their needs. They will feel special. It takes time but not necessarily money – there's much here that makes smarter use of existing material.

Maximising empathy starts with looking at how think-ing big can shape your personalised communications.

'Know my business' = commercial closeness

This is what clients say – 'Know my business'.

In the introduction, I said, 'You will know the names of the people who matter, or it's easy to find them.'

To show that you care, you should know your priority organisations and people *as well as they know them-selves*. I mean really care, not pretend 'care', driven by the hollow motive of financial gain. In *The Relationship Revolution*, Larry Hochman calls this knowledge 'com-mercial closeness'.[40] You will have experienced it on a small scale say when you walk into your regular cafe and the person behind the counter knows what you want. Better still, they got it ready when you joined the queue. Or perhaps you've gone to a meeting and the receptionist didn't just sign you in without mak-ing eye contact and hand over a badge. Instead, they welcomed you, used your name, gave you a pre-prepared badge, knew who you'd come to see, and, perhaps, recalled something relevant about you. That

---

40 Hochman, *The Relationship Revolution*.

H2H (Human to Human) spark is now so rare that you don't just notice it – you *feel* it.

Technology makes commercial closeness very easy.

Marketing Director of top-50 law firm, on commercial closeness:

> 'We used the Propella methodology with a well-established team who thought they "knew everything" about their clients. By the end of the day, new thoughts and plans on those relationships were in place. These have all led to new business beyond everyone's expectations.'

So much information is now available on your VIPs and Upgraders that it is absolutely possible to know what's going on outside and often inside their organisations.

Listen big and listen small. Ask the right questions and look for the answers (sometimes between the lines – I've written enough corporate statements to spot what vital information is obvious by its exclusion). Look for connections and they will come.

To partner with the VIPs and find the common ground with Upgraders, you need to know what that organisation or person wants or needs that will make their lives easier – what might save them money, give them more time, accelerate their plans, boost their career, make them look good. And, this is important, it may *not* relate directly to your brand or services.

Think of yourself as a connector between them and what they want. Their want/to-do list is *your* list of possibilities that warrant constant attention.

It's powerful to open up bespoke communication with something like:

'Your news release on the XYZ appointment mentioned you were looking for similar acquisitions in France and Spain. I've got two contacts you might be interested in...'

'Last time we spoke, you mentioned that you were short of experts who could do X, Y, and Z. I've found someone who could fill that gap...'

'You came to our event on ABC and the associate who sat with you thought you might need some specific help on blah blah blah...'

I will always, always, find a way to help a client identify and follow up on the golden opportunity.

Listen big, below, gives you an idea of where to look for your clues and cues.

Listen big

Bespoke communications need to start with something about them. Here are some ideas and places to look for inspiration on the opening lines.

- Set up a Google Alert for them so you know their every public announcement and are aware of anything said about them on social media. Respond to news, both positive and negative. If they appoint someone new, win an award, or come top in a league table, congratulate them and share their success. If it's negative news, think about offering your moral and practical support. You might, for example, know someone who has been through a similar situation. Or you might know an expert who can help. The offer, if not your idea, can be appreciated.

- What are their numbers? Turnover. Profit. Share price. Daily trends. Industry positions. Market share. Best-selling products. Number of employees. Number of offices. Key dates. Competitor activity. Read their announcements. Closely. Read between the lines, too.

- Study and decipher their website. What are their messages? How are they positioning themselves? Where is the common ground? If, for example, they are positioning themselves as an international business, it makes sense, in communications with them, to promote your international credentials. What are their stated ambitions? Who are the leaders? Who is on the board? Who are the executive directors? Who is on the management team? If you don't know the name of a particular person, it can often be found via the company's LinkedIn page, or in an organisation chart buried in the website. Or, phone up and ask. What are their corporate-responsibility priorities? What are their diversity credentials?

Who is associated with them? What are their priorities and policies? If, for example, they have a policy of promoting women, you might choose a trailblazing woman from your team to lead the relationship. What news are they pushing out? Look closely at quotes from the CEO and other important people. What are they saying in the annual reports or other showcase documents? What are they telling shareholders? What are their competitors saying and doing?

This information is invaluable in helping you to shape your communications around what *they need to hear* to *find the common ground*.

Law firm A wanted to position its food-sector team credentials to a major food producer (a Prize). By studying the news on their website, we found a series of press releases announcing recent acquisitions and their stated ambition to look for similar businesses in a particular geography. Law firm A presented its food-sector offering to this business leading on its M&A credentials, sector, and location contacts.

A financial services company sells planning and investment services to employees in a particular sector. By studying the recruitment sections of target websites, we were able to identify which organisations valued the financial and family well-being of their people. Instead of leading with the traditional 'we are marvellous' sales message, the company focused on how their products and services could support this HR policy.

You cannot fail to impress by demonstrating how much you know about a sector, an organisation, or a person in your opening lines of any conversation or communication.

- What do people look like? See how they present themselves online by searching Google Images. You can find out a lot about people's attitudes, preferences, and outlook on life this way – and then you match your message.

- Follow the organisation on LinkedIn and occasionally respond to what you see through likes, shares, and comments.

- Connect with people in the organisation and notice their online activity. Show an interest. Like and comment on their posts. Look for connections (what they're following, trends, interests). If you think this is a step too far, remember, they've *chosen* to post these things in the public domain. That said, you need to be diplomatic. I once researched a high-profile woman I was due to sit next to at a dinner. Her social media profile revealed she had recently enjoyed the erotic novel *Fifty Shades of Grey*. I declined to mention that over dinner!

- In your CRM system or phone, note openly available information, such as important names, dates, and numbers, so that it's always on hand.

- Track the relevant media and sector associations to stay on top of trends and developments. When you read newspapers, be mindful of news which may provide insights you can share with a VIP or Upgrader.

- For VIP organisations, introduce a client-service review. Ask open questions that trigger information-sharing. This will allow you to spot ongoing partnering opportunities.

To learn how to stand in the shoes of their clients or targets, Propella workshop participants complete a 24-hour clock outlining their client's day. This is when they realise that when they're not directly engaged in a project with that client, they occupy a very small part, if any, of that person's life. Commercial closeness helps you to stay on the frontline by being useful.

If you still think commercial closeness doesn't matter, remember this story. When reducing their legal panel, one listed client called in all the panel firms to a theatre-style meeting and asked them to write down the organisation's share price at the close of play the previous day, their top-selling product, and the number of employees. Firms unable to answer the questions were asked to leave the room. Panel selection complete. Using criteria critical to your top clients, how would you fare?

When you see the world from the organisation's end of the telescope, you can communicate with them in a way that sparks a connection. Commercial closeness makes it easy to...

... Be useful (no, be completely and utterly indispensable)

Think beyond the obvious to see where you can add real value. There is *always* an easy but highly valued, hugely memorable 'give' that will delight.

- Introductions to valuable connections – Ensure you are well connected and a good networker. Think about networking as something you do for other people, not for yourself, and a whole new world of possibilities opens up.

- Associations/partnerships – Can you smooth the path for your VIP/Upgrader to build a relationship or partnership with a third party?

- Sales opportunities – You may come by some intelligence that someone is looking for the exact services your VIP/Upgrader provides.

- Merger opportunities – Your contact may have signalled that they're looking to merge, and your market intelligence could deliver some candidates. You may know exactly the right person to ask.

- Suppliers – If your VIP/Upgrader is looking for a new supplier, can you recommend someone?

- Recruitment or staff needs – They may be looking for a particular person or skill set, something out of the ordinary, and you could locate that person by scanning your network.

- Training or speaker requests – Are they looking for a trainer or expert to come into their business, say for a team awayday, and you know just the person? You may even be able to do it yourself.

- Industry information – Have they signalled interest in a particular industry? And can you link that to anything you might receive in your inbox, an industry expert in your organisation, or something that you spot in a magazine?

- Sector knowledge – Secure a good source of sector intelligence, one that offers vertical and horizontal information relevant to your needs. It's incredibly satisfying to drop an information gem into a conversation.

- Competitor information – A competitor of your VIP/Upgrader has announced something significant. How can you help your VIP/Upgrader respond?

When you focus on a small number of organisations and people, the most amazing opportunities will emerge. Become the 'mastermind' of your VIPs/Upgraders. They should be your specialist subject. Share your findings within your organisation and ask colleagues to share what information they pick up. Propella is a team game.

The closer you get to the organisation and the people, the more opportunities are created to listen to what they really want. You will reach a point in the relationship when you can just ask them how you might add the most value. Eventually, you won't need to ask. You'll be in their circle of trust and they'll simply let you know what they need.

Become indispensable.

Commenting on their client partner in a client-service review, one in-house lawyer said, 'She knows what I want before I do.' This is the Holy Grail comment.

This is not about waiting for them to contact you with the next piece of work. This is about creating the next opportunity to be *involved* with that work.

Mark Cooper is General Counsel and Company Secretary for Cadent, which owns, manages, and operates four of the UK's eight gas distribution networks in a highly regulated industry. He leads a 25-person-strong team of lawyers, company secretarial specialists, auditors, risk specialists, and support staff. His team is supported by a panel of six law firms. Mark has worked in private practice and has first-hand experience of responsibility for winning and retaining business.

His thoughts on best-practice communications from law firms are in the context of the demands and priorities working in-house: 'Some firms assume we always have the time to get a coffee. We appreciate the invitations but there should be something to catch up on. The best firms have a good understanding of our focus and priorities and tailor their approach.'

- On legal briefings and updates: 'If we are sent too much from a firm, we may end up ignoring it. The best firms send us filtered material now and then. We appreciate it when the firm has clearly thought about how it might be relevant to us.'

- On brand awareness/marketing initiatives: 'Credibility is a base layer to the relationship: we welcome being given the heads-up if one of our firms is leading on or responding to a topical media story or is sponsoring an industry event. If it is relevant to our business, it demonstrates that the firm really understands us.'

- On managing multiple stakeholders: 'Our law firms need to maintain a good relationship with the in-house legal team. On day-to-day projects, they may need to extend that relationship to other teams such as Property, IT, Procurement or HR. No one likes to be surprised, so it is worth identifying all relevant stakeholders at an early stage and keeping them updated on relevant developments.'

- On pushy sales from off-panel firms: 'We rarely go off panel. We are governed by the procurement regulations and have invested time in appointing the right advisers to our current panel. A pushy sales approach backfires. The best firms understand the bigger picture and take a longer-term view.'

Nail the opportunities closer to home

Think about your VIPs and Upgraders. What is the nature of their interactions with your organisation? Who do they talk with and what have they said? Switching from broadcasting to observing and listening reveals hidden opportunities. People drop clues *all* the time about what they want. What marketing events have they attended? What initiatives have they shown interest in? If people are spending time at your events or visiting your website, they are there for a reason.

Are you tracking these visits? How are you capturing and acting upon this interest? I am amazed by how many professional firms fail to see the potential business right under their noses. Their clients and targets are virtually saying 'help me out here'.

Accountancy firm C wanted to build its entrepreneur client base. This firm had a track record with plenty of Ambassadors, and the goal was to win twenty new entrepreneurial clients in the following twelve months. Before diving into the unknown, they explored *existing* marketing information and discovered there were over 600 (and rising) unique visitors on the entrepreneurial section of their website *every quarter*. All they had to do was introduce a consensual data-capture incentive, filter on criteria, and hey presto – they had a rich potential client list of Upgraders right up against the 50 on the Loyalty axis.

Clients are often very proud of their event success and point to the number of attendees as a success measure (output). Yet, they can't tell me about new business won as a result of that event (outcome). One firm, on sharing their impressive guest list for their quarterly employment-law breakfast briefings, showed me how some HR personnel from target clients regularly travelled long distances in the rush hour to attend. Yet, despite it being obvious that those people were virtually saying 'help me, my current advisers aren't giving me this information', they never followed up with them. It was seen as too pushy, too 'salesy'. Task number one when they returned to their desks that day was to pick up the phone and begin a meaningful dialogue with those attendees.

Even in a client-service review designed for 100% listening and feedback, a client will often hint at a new business opportunity for you to pick up. If the relationship is operating at full trust, sometimes they might share a problem not even realising you have the solution.

The head of a chambers Family Law team commissioned a third-party client-service review with the head of large family law firm. The team felt they had some good relationships with VIPs at the firm, but a large number of Upgrader junior lawyers were instructing other sets. It emerged during the interview that the biggest challenge for the head of the team wasn't how to give more work to this chambers – it was how to deal with a forthcoming shortfall, as several junior lawyers were going on maternity leave. The set stepped in to provide temporary support and a new stage of the relationship began. A complete win-win.

'Know my country, know my culture'

Whoever said that 'England and America are two countries separated by the same language' (commonly believed to be George Bernard Shaw) could not have imagined today's global reality. Most businesses have clients, targets, networks, contacts, and employees way beyond their own countries. Working with international clients means personalisation is essential.

Nigel Ewington, founder of TCO International, a consultancy that accelerates global agility, works with organisations whose operations spread across different countries and cultures.[41] His workshops with large groups of mixed nationalities achieve astonishing levels of self-realisation. Building on the work of anthropologist and cross-cultural researcher Edward T. Hall,[42] Nigel, in a personal interview for this book, explains how recipients respond to communication in high- and low-context cultures:

> 'In high-context cultures, such as South East Asia, Southern Europe, and the Middle East, there is an assumption that real effective communication happens by focusing on context, empathising with and understanding

---

41 Contact Nigel Ewington through TCO's website: http://www.tco-international.com/.

42 Edward T. Hall, *The Silent Language* (New York, NY: Anchor Books, 1959).

another's situation, feelings, and motives. Here there is a need to show respect to clients by investing in closer relationships, deeper levels of personal trust, and richer channels of communication, particularly large amounts of face-to-face time, the highest-context channel of communication.

'In low-context cultures, such as the USA, Germany, and the Nordic countries, there is a sense that effective communication is about focusing on text, "what" they actually say, not so much "how", "when", and "where" they say it, and being simple, precise, and clear. This may mean that respect is shown less by close relationships but [more] by asking the right questions and by giving a clear, efficient explanation of the benefits you offer. This may include digitising online questionnaires to support the sales process and avoid wasting the customer's precious time.'

Straight away, you can see how different communication approaches will be required depending on whether you're communicating with someone in a high-context country or a low-context country.

An extra dimension to consider when planning content and approach is the difference between **universalist** and **particularist** cultures.

Nigel Ewington says,

> 'In universalist cultures, people are more
> likely to accept that the same universal rules
> that apply to everyone else apply equally to
> them, and they will judge negatively anything
> that violates this. Clients are happy to be
> treated like everyone else. They will follow the
> contract they have signed or the arrangement
> agreed as it guarantees a kind of universal
> quality and is in the best interests of all parties.
>
> 'In particularist countries, people tend to
> expect to be treated in a "particular" way
> because of circumstances and relationships,
> despite what the rules say and sometimes
> despite the conflicting needs of others. Clients
> need to be made to feel special, and receive a
> priority service. The contract or arrangement is
> only a starting point for a discussion of needs.'

Practical guidance

- Apply the right tone of voice (e.g. soft and deferential for Japan vs assertive for Germany)

- Be mindful of perceived differences in concepts regarding the relative status of service provider and client

- Build in flexible and face-to-face time for clients in high-context countries but respect the efficiency and time allocation expected by those in low-context countries

- Use the right degree of formality (first name vs titled name)

- Avoid over-stereotyping people based on where they come from. What is personal to one person is different for another person, even if they're from the same cultural background. Take into account age, position in relation to you, and status

- Be mindful of religious holidays and special days in other cultures

- English may be the accepted business language, but when possible, use the recipient's language. Nigel Ewington: 'Language is a key component of a person's identity. When you choose to communicate with someone in their own language, they have more of an emotional association with the words and a richer vocabulary for describing and interpreting their needs.'

Now that your radar is extended to the big picture, we'll look at how small acts of personalisation can produce beautiful results.

CHAPTER THIRTEEN

Act Small (With Beautiful Results)

'Just as ripples spread out when a single pebble is dropped into water, the actions of individuals can have far-reaching effects.'
— The Dalai Lama

In Chapter 12, we explored how thinking big can inform your communications. In this chapter, we'll uncover the impact of small actions. By impact, I mean it could be an incoming phone call, coffee, lunch, meeting, a 'please could you let me have your views', whatever, even an instruction, a brief, a job… but it's all about achieving that elusive face-to-face (F2F) marketing and more work. This is a world apart from the background noise/'keep them informed' approach designed for standard stakeholders. Instead this will elicit a response and keep people moving towards the 100 on your Loyalty axis.

Standing in the client's shoes (or whoever it is you want to reach), here are my seven personalisation no-brainers for kick-starting a conversation:

- Know my name (and have a good opening line that speaks to me)

- Keep your priority stakeholders one step ahead

- Be interested – it's priceless (and channel Michael McIntyre)

- The power of private dining

- Capitalise on generosity of spirit (your greatest untapped resource)

- Show me the real you

And the most important of all:

- Find your own Power of Personal

'Know my name' (and have a good opening line that speaks to me)

'Remember that a person's name is, to that person, the sweetest and most important sound in any language.'[43]

In *How to Win Friends and Influence People* (written in 1936 and still a bestseller), Dale Carnegie highlights the value of names. He developed the LIRA formula for remembering them: Look and Listen, Impression, Repetition, Association.

Something special occurs when we hear our name, but why?

Content strategist Erik Devaney, in *The Psychology of Personalization: Why We Crave Customized Experiences*,[44] refers to a University of Texas study that attributes human preference for personalised experience to 'two key factors – desire for control and information overload'.[45] If a recipient receives something tailored to them, they

43 Dale Carnegie, *How to Win Friends and Influence People* (New York, NY: Simon and Schuster, 1936).

44 Erik Devaney, 'The Psychology of Personalization: Why We Crave Customised Experiences', HubSpot, last updated 9 August 2017. https://blog.hubspot.com/marketing/psychology-personalization.

45 Laura Frances Bright, 'Consumer Control and Customization in Online Environments: An Investigation into the Psychology of Consumer Choice and its Impact on Media Enjoyment, Attitude, and Behavioral Intention', PhD Dissertation, University of Texas at Austin, December 2008. https://repositories.lib.utexas.edu/handle/2152/18054.

feel more in control. Personalisation can reduce the feeling of being overwhelmed by information because it's a more manageable framework for engagement.

Devaney points to the brain's reticular activating system (RAS), the gateway that information passes through to reach the brain and that filters information so the person pays attention to the right things. Referring to a study published in *Brain Research*, he says, 'When people hear their own first name… there is a unique reaction in the brain.'[46] Of course there is – you're talking to me! You have my attention. My RAS kicks in and important information rises above the noise.

I like all these theories, but I generally go with the view that addressing someone by their name is respectful, complimentary, and good manners, especially if there has been previous engagement.

Think about the people with whom you choose to spend your time and money or give your support. You will respond positively when a real person has made an effort to communicate with you as a real person, a fellow human being. Think about how you like to be treated by suppliers and contacts. You want to be recognised, acknowledged, thought of, put first, and made to feel important.

---

46 Dennis P. Carmody and Michael Lewis, 'Brain Activation When Hearing One's Own and Others' Names', *Brain Research*, 1116/1 (20 October 2006), 153–58. https://www.ncbi.nlm.nih.gov/pmc/articles/PMC1647299/.

© marketoonist.com

Some of the most successful leaders I've seen during live presentations or in videos use names of people in the audience. They may supplement the name with a relevant story (name + story = communications success). Those public references are magnified by the named people to their peer groups and social networks. Ambassadors are created in an instant. Others are motivated to want a spot in that limelight.

Some presenters are gifted with the skill of making people feel as if they are being spoken to individually (Bill Clinton and Barack Obama are said to have this skill in shedloads). We know when we've been on the receiving end of that skill, and it leaves a lasting impression.

If you need to get past a secretary, PA, or other gate-keeper, a good starting point is to find out and use their name. Some people think that person and their name are unimportant, yet they're actually the most important if you ever want to get through.

With any communications, after using the person's name it's important to have a relevant opening line. Choose something that refers to a previous conversation or to something that you know is important to them. (See commercial closeness in Chapter 12.)

Bespoke your marketing emails to VIPs and Upgraders. That means changing the first few lines and checking that the rest is *bullseye* relevant to the reader. Make them think the whole thing is created for them. 'Write for your reader' is the first technique in Scott Keyser's *rhetorica*®:

> 'When we focus on ourselves, the connection
> with the reader is weak. But when we shift
> our focus to the reader, something magical
> happens. Our language changes. We
> automatically use the magic words "you"
> and "your". Content centres on the benefits
> to the reader of our product, service… The
> connection with the reader is strong.'[47]

---

47 Keyser, *rhetorica*®.

Absolutely everything you send to your VIPs and Upgraders should start with 'You' or 'Your', not the automatic 'I', 'We', or 'Our'. Some examples:

You will have heard that…

You mentioned that…

You popped into my head today when I saw…

Your company was recently in the news about XYZ, and we thought you might be interested in…

Your colleague Fred Bloggs mentioned to me that…

Your name came up in a conversation the other day about XYZ, and we thought you were exactly the right person for…

You have previously said that if ever we organised an event in such-a-such location, you wanted to be the first to know…

You are one of the few people I know who would be really interested in this, given that…

You and I talked last time about…

Derek Allen Mason, founding director of Super Structures Associates, a niche structural engineering company, used this technique in a marketing campaign to promote his book, *Will It Stand Up?*,[48] to his professional network. The middle few paragraphs of his letter were standard, but the opening and closing paragraphs were tailored to each recipient. The emphasis in the text was how the lessons in the book could help them with their projects. Derek signed each letter and book personally. The mailing was staggered to ensure that Ambassadors, Prizes, and Boomerangs received the first versions.

Derek:

'Everybody on my mailing list was known to me. Many of us had worked together and some of us had become good friends. All I did was reference the personal relationship in the opening paragraph, changed the call to action and put my signature on the bottom, some with a PS, which included calls to action and personal reminders that we should meet up soon to have a catch-up and see how we could help each other. It is the personal touch and showing a genuine interest in people that has driven the success of this campaign.'

---

48   Derek Mason, *Will It Stand Up? A Professional Engineer's View of the Creation of the London 2012 Olympic Stadium* (Gorleston: Rethink Press, 2017).

Keep your priority stakeholders one step ahead

On cost (time and money) vs benefit, when it comes to personalised marketing tools, the most popular (eventually[49]) is in-advance communication of otherwise standard communications tools with a bespoke email or letter. Regular choices include press releases (embargoed), articles, event invitations, and reports. These opportunities are gifts for partnering with VIPs and finding common ground with Upgraders.

Build in an extra few days (or hours if pressure is on) before the announcement or mailing to send a personal communication that, by its very nature, places a value on the relationship. Not everything needs to be last minute. Starting with the standard email or letter prepared by you or your marketing adviser, bespoke the opening paragraph and sign-off line (usually a call to action) for each recipient. To do that, you have to mentally reconnect to that person; think about your recent conversations, refresh your commercial closeness intelligence, stand in their shoes and think about your message from their point of view. Sometimes it will feel as if one part of your brain is transmitting

---

49   Resistance (and I'm being polite here) is the first reaction when I
      suggest this approach to clients. However, despite the initial time
      and brainpower involved, clients are so pleasantly surprised with
      the results that they look forward to repeating it and improving their
      score. Once you're in the personalisation mindset, it will get quicker
      and easier with practice and positive feedback.

impulses to another part as you mentally connect your recipient with the news you're about to share. When it happens, you'll feel that spark. The recipient will know that you are talking to them directly, and only them. They will feel the spark. Your communication stands out above the others. It is not discarded. It is respected. The connection has been made and they will respond. Even if you only manage to bespoke your communications to a few people, the impact is disproportionately high to the effort involved. Financial cost is a blissful zero.

Here are three real-life examples that generated F2F opportunities. Also note the sign-off call to action.

Appointment press release

You will remember last time we met, I mentioned the team was in the early stages of recruiting a top-five person with blah blah blah expertise. I thought that person would be a good fit for your blah blah blah project. I was sworn to secrecy then so unable to share the details, but now that I can, I wanted you to be the first to know that XYZ is joining us from ABC, and here is an advance copy of the press release.

If you'd like to meet XYZ, let me know and I'll arrange that for the first week.

Event invitation

You are one of a small selection of people we thought might be interested in a breakfast we're hosting on 5 June. ABC speaker has agreed to present, and because there are only twenty places for guests, I wanted to give you advance notice so we could reserve a seat for you.

Let me know if you want one of the places so I can put your name on the list.

Country report

You have always expressed an interest in how Africa is shaping up as an emerging economy, especially in relation to your blah blah plans. We're just about to publish a new report that confirms your optimism and highlights which African countries are forging ahead and why. I wanted you to see this before it goes out far and wide, so please find enclosed an advance copy.

Our African expert made some interesting contacts while researching the report. If you'd like to catch up with us both, let me know and I'll put something in the diary before she gets too busy.

In-advance distribution of press releases to VIPs and Upgraders, with a bespoke email from the managing partner, accelerated the reputational success of the then newly opened London office of US litigation powerhouse Boies Schiller Flexner. All case success and appointment press releases were sent out to a small number of clients, targets, and contacts with a personal email from managing partner Natasha Harrison *before* they were sent to the media or published on the firm's website. They were also sent to recruitment consultants to improve the chances of their recommending a relatively unknown brand as a career choice to the City's elite litigation and arbitration lawyers seeking a new challenge.

Natasha Harrison, managing partner of Boies Schiller Flexner (UK):

'*At the time, we were carving out a niche for ourselves in a highly competitive and crowded market. Sending out bespoke emails with our news was hard work and time-consuming, especially to people who barely knew us in the UK and had existing relationships with established firms. Writing those emails was something only I could do, and it was an additional task on an already busy typical managing partner's schedule. In the early days, those golden opportunities are rare and I knew we had to make the most of them if our capability and progress was going to reach the right people. The first time was on our success in the Canary Wharf litigation, where we applied a rarely used legal principle to help secure a £169 million refund, plus interest, for our clients. Each email about the case success came from me personally and finished with a suggestion to meet for coffee or lunch. I found that people really appreciated being told about the background and developments before everyone else and, most important of all, they were curious and accepted the coffee and lunch invitations. It opened the right doors for us at just the right time and helped us to become an established City legal brand ahead of schedule.*'

Be interested – it's priceless

After the big sell, the biggest complaint I hear from clients and colleagues, friends, contacts, people chatting on social media, etc. buying high-value services is the lack of interest shown by the professional(s) they eventually deal with further down the line. We've all experienced it. That complaint applies across the board, from simple conveyancing and personal tax work to the full range of high-end commercial services.

After all that effort to win the work, a professional – someone who doesn't understand the monumental effort involved in winning business – turns up in front of the newly impressed client and lets the side down. It may be the 400th time that person has done a particular piece of work, but to the client it may be the *first and only* time they ever buy this advice. It might be a distress purchase (divorce, litigation, tax mitigation, professional negligence) with a risk attached, or a landmark life/business moment (registering a trademark, buying or selling a business or second home, or finalising a pension scheme). Professionals are often unaware that their attitude is conveying utter boredom and negativity combined with a wall of administration when a client is expecting interest, positivity, and a 'let's do this' attitude. There can be a baffling mismatch of expectations.

There are many techniques to overcome this, but here's my solution if you think it might apply to people in your business.

Channel comedian Michael McIntyre (or his equivalent in your country). If you don't know him, watch him on YouTube.

Michael McIntyre walks on stage with a sense of purpose, enormous energy and enthusiasm. He is 100% *interested* in pleasing his audience and delivers his sketches to perfection. His audience laughs, and he laughs with them. We all laugh *even* if we've seen them before. Yet, Michael McIntyre has rehearsed those sketches hundreds if not thousands of times. He must be bored brainless by them, but the audience would never know.

Michael McIntyre is reported to be the highest-grossing comedian in the world.

All clients deserve positivity and a can-do attitude. All are potential Ambassadors and can recommend to others. They might go on to buy additional services. Some private clients will be buyers of business advice and vice versa.

The power of private dining

An underused but exquisite event format is the small, discreet private dining event in a gorgeous location. There is something fundamentally human about the sharing of food that spans countries, cultures, and generations. To see word of mouth in action, mix VIPs and Upgraders, seat an Ambassador next to a Prize, or work with your Trojan Horse internal Ambassador to woo an Upgrader. Put together guests from different organisations but who have a shared interest.

The exclusive nature of the private dining format makes it a more meaningful social interaction. Choose something special, such as a chef's table, or private dining facilities in a new or highly sought-after restaurant. Be original – choose unusual places closed off to the wider public. Who wouldn't enjoy a dinner in the iconic Sir John Soane's Museum (or any one of the eighty-one similar venues available in London for dinner parties of thirty people)? There will be similar places wherever you are. Be respectful regarding different cultural expectations, attitudes to alcohol, religious days, and food philosophies.

The choice of venue should align with the guest's status and place in their hierarchy. You could present a top-industry speaker or arrange a Chatham House Rule debate chaired by a third party. Invite a leading journalist or influencer in the sector, subject to Chatham House Rule, to contribute and open up relationship-building opportunities.

There really is more to this type of communal eating than refuelling.

In his article *Breaking Bread: the Functions of Social Eating*, Robin Dunbar, Emeritus Professor of Evolutionary Psychology at University of Oxford, writes:

> 'Evening meals that result in respondents feeling closer to those with whom they eat involve more people, more laughter and reminiscing, as well as alcohol. A path analysis suggests that the causal direction runs from eating together to bondedness rather than the other way around. Social eating may have evolved as a mechanism for facilitating social bonding.'[50]

Other benefits of a private dining event:

- A safe, closed environment encourages more meaningful conversation, and this is attractive to senior people.

- The right guests will perceive its value from the start.

---

50 Robin Dunbar, 'Breaking Bread: the Functions of Social Eating in Adaptive Human Behaviour and Physiology', *Adaptive Human Behavior and Physiology*, 3/3 (September 2017).

- It can position you and your organisation as thought leaders.

- Guests will feel it's worthy of their time because their presence will be visible (ditto their absence).

- Because they are visible among their peers, people will ask questions and participate (rather than sit back and listen, in receive mode). Taking part makes it a more meaningful experience.

- You can collect new intelligence that will give you easy next steps.

- Guests who have hosted similar events will value the same hospitality being shown to them. Some of our clients have found these dinners so successful that their guests now host their own.

- The right venue will make it a memorable occasion that they will talk about to others.

- They will remember it better than any presentation.

- They will come again. Loyalty secured.

It can also be used *alongside* big-piece conferences or events. Try inviting a small number of VIP/Upgrader delegates to a private dining experience before or after a big-piece event. If your VIPs and Upgraders are somewhere for a conference, capitalise on their availability.

Events specialist Judie Caunce, of Events Plus – Painless and Professional Corporate Events, has organised hundreds of events for professional services firms and membership associations.

> 'Private dinners are an excellent way of putting together like-minded people in a convivial atmosphere to build trust and understanding. Clients often tell us that the person they have 'known' for years, they didn't really know at all until they were sitting together at a private dining event. Smaller numbers also open up the possibilities of different venues – not faceless hotels but quirky or rarely accessible or historical gems in the host city, which adds to the sense of being part of something special and, therefore, a highly valued guest.'

Chambers A realised they were only receiving work from a small percentage of partners – their Ambassadors – in a particular law firm. This work was declining, as some Ambassadors were retiring. On closer inspection, they discovered that junior partners and associates in the firm's team had the authority to instruct counsel, and this work was going to Chamber A's competition. Their Propella map presented a classic result – a couple of Ambassadors and a few VIPs but a large number of Upgrader people. Chambers A had neglected the next generation. While there was still a window of opportunity, Chambers A organised a private dining event in the law firm's city and invited their Ambassadors, VIPs, and Upgraders. Although the dinner was hosted by the QC leading the team, Chambers A was largely represented by A's juniors. Guest research led to a seating plan where people with shared interests were sat next to each other. Result: new relationships were formed that led to more work being referred.

Generosity of spirit (your greatest untapped resource)

'Attention is the rarest and purest form of generosity.'
— Simone Weil

I don't mean this in a hippy-dippy sense. Generosity of spirit is about being willing – without being asked or told – to give more of something (money, time, or skill) than is expected – without expecting something in return. It cannot be faked. These are Larry Hochman's 'small kindnesses.'[51] Sometimes the term used is Random Acts of Kindness, or RAKs. I think thoughtfulness not thoughtlessness.

Generosity of spirit demonstrates confidence and is an attractive, magnetic quality. Readers of this book will almost certainly be sitting on a mountain of value in the generosity they can show to others. It's also very now. Generosity of spirit is highly valued by Millennials.

---

51 Hochman, *The Relationship Revolution.*

In *Give and Take: A Revolutionary Approach to Success*, a *New York Times* and *Wall Street Journal* bestseller, Adam Grant introduces two types of people at opposite ends of the reciprocity spectrum: givers and takers, with matchers in the middle.

> 'If we want to succeed, we need a combination of hard work, talent, and luck. [Yet there is] a fourth ingredient, one that's critical but often neglected: success depends heavily on how we approach our interactions with other people. Every time we interact with another person at work, we have a choice to make: do we try to claim as much value as we can, or contribute value without worrying about what we receive in return?'[52]

The book goes on to explain how and why givers are the winners and that giving matters more now than ever.

Whenever I talk about generosity of spirit to clients, almost everyone can recall at least one occasion when the experience has happened to them, family or friends. And then they realise they have the power to make it happen for others. Such giving can be inexpensive and easy.

---

52 A. Grant, *Give and Take: A Revolutionary Approach to Success* (London: Weidenfeld & Nicolson, 2013).

Generosity of spirit includes the concept of 'paying it forward', which now has its own day (28 April) recognised in eighty-five countries.

Being thoughtful delivers the most beautiful results. It's deeply meaningful to the recipient in an impersonal world. It creates a sense of delight above and beyond a commercial transaction. One act of thoughtfulness can last a long time. Opportunities for thoughtfulness are rare, which is why it's important to tune into them.

Thoughtfulness is unique to the recipient – that's the point – but here are some suggestions.

- Say thank you for work given. For long-standing or repeat clients, there should be some acknowledgement of loyalty.

- Share information (not confidential information) that is outside the normal. This is a precious gift, especially if it's highly personalised and for the exclusive use of the recipient.

- Send, share, or recommend books on a subject they may have mentioned, especially new titles. The gift of knowledge is always welcome. Ditto articles, reports, and thought-leadership papers sent in the post with a handwritten note, or emailed from you.

- Recognise, take into account, and act upon the individual significance of religious festivals, holy days, and observances.

- Cater for special dietary requirements, if made known to you. Well done that firm which provided the gluten-free lunch to a coeliac client on the second visit *without* being prompted. I know of one law firm client who switched from another law firm, on the basis of exceptional out-of-hours catering enjoyed during an all-nighter corporate transaction when they had been on the other side.

- Acknowledge birthdays, anniversaries, holidays, and personal circumstances (*if* mentioned to you). If someone tells you that they need to leave a meeting to see a family member in hospital, ask about that person next time you see them. If someone tells you that their kids are taking exams and it's all a bit tense at home, make a diary note to ask about the results. If someone tells you that they're going on holiday to a place you know, recommend the best restaurants. Teeny-tiny things can make a difference. Common sense will tell you not to store this type of personal information in a database – it's something thoughtful you recall when you next speak to them. GDPR dictates that you must not store sensitive information such as health details or political opinions without explicit consent. There is nothing wrong with knowing this information but do not store that information in your firm's client database either on paper or electronically.

- Be an Ambassador for them. Attend their events, support their corporate responsibility, and back their issues. Make introductions and share contacts.

- Remember details of their relationship with you, like what they have bought or referred before. You may have forgotten the details. They will not.

- Pay suppliers before the due date.

- Upcycle something that you no longer have a use for but that will make a difference to someone else's life.

Thoughtfulness isn't about owning people and having them in your debt. Neither is it about spending huge amounts of money. In fact, contemporary thoughtfulness definitely does not cost large amounts of money. Increasingly, clients would rather you contribute to the world's more meaningful problems than provide them with entertainment.

These examples of thoughtfulness are all small and relatively cost free. Indeed, the cost of thoughtlessness can be far greater. Here's a story about an expensive bottle of champagne never bought.

My favourite example of expensive thoughtlessness relates to a small luxury seaside hotel run by a husband and wife team. Every year for several years, some friends stayed in this hotel on a two-week, blow-the-budget holiday for two adults, four teenage children, and eventually their girlfriends and boyfriends. At the end of each stay, they would automatically rebook for the same two weeks the following year. Then one year, the husband and wife owners never acknowledged the return of this family. In fact, when they arrived, they were treated as if they had never been there before. There was no welcome-back note, no 'here is your favourite table', no complimentary bottle of champagne, nada. That was their last trip. All that guaranteed income gone for the cost of a little thought and the price of some champagne.

What it's not

Note that there's a fine line between thoughtfulness and looking like a stalker and/or a sycophant. Don't go there. Ever.

A Greek CEO told me about one accountant who tried to secure a face-to-face meeting with him by having Greek pastries, accompanied by the firm's brochure, delivered to his office daily. No. That's stalking and off-the-scale needy. Surprisingly, he never took her calls. But the security guys enjoyed the pastries!

Neither is it about being matey or showing off. I've known professionals who go to the ends of the earth to buy front-row tickets for sporting and music events just to impress clients. Fine, but…

- It's all a bit obvious, a bit standard, a bit easy. Your competitors can offer the same.

- You invariably end up in a crowd.

- It's tricky meeting the needs of both men and women.

- Care needs to be taken not to stray into personal territory and be seen as offering favours.

- It can all go horribly wrong if there's alcohol involved. Alcohol is off limits for some people.

- Some clients can very obviously afford their own front-row tickets to the events they want to attend.

- It can cost a huge amount of money, especially per person, take up a chunk of marketing budget, and comes with an obligation to repeat it.

- Some organisations have strict rules about bribery regulations.

Show me the real you

Two underused but highly effective means of communication easily at your disposal are handwriting and telephone calls. Both deliver impact that far outweighs the effort involved. Both represent something tangible and exclusive from the sender.

Handwriting

Handwriting is powerful because it's the polar opposite of a commodity communication. Your words in your own writing give something deliberately of yourself that's unique, thoughtful, and authentic. It cannot be faked. Graphology is the science behind this. In *Handwriting: An Instrument of Understanding and Empathy*, Simon Esposito says,

> 'The line of ink left by the pen forms the layout or "graphic wire" which, if carefully examined, makes possible an understanding of the characteristics of the personality and the attitudes of the writer.'[53]

Personally sign the communications you send to priority contacts, perhaps with a sign-off line that demonstrates you thought about the recipient. The

---

53 S. Esposito, 'Handwriting: An Instrument of Understanding and Empathy', *SymMel*, 11 (2015).

salutation can also be handwritten. Even on standard direct mail, a nice touch is to handwrite a postscript to show that there was some human contact before the document went in the envelope.

Have a stationery wardrobe. Equip yourself with some quality notepaper cards, paper, and envelopes, or order some pre-printed cards with your name and number across the top and proper matching envelopes. You could commission some postcards, perhaps with quotes or images that mean something to your organisation. Thank-you/thinking-of-you/congratulations/good-luck notes also work brilliantly. Use a good pen (we've all got a few special birthday pens stashed away somewhere)!

Devote ten minutes of your day (small ask) to handwriting something to someone. That's probably less time than you spend on social media or in a boring meeting, and it will have far more impact. Recipients often keep handwritten notes, so it's a communication that will keep on giving.

Formal communications, such as terms of engagement, invoices, contracts, etc., are undervalued touchpoints that often make an unwelcome landing on a client's desk or in their inbox. Adding a handwritten compliment slip or, for online communications, a bespoke email can mitigate their sterility. My theory is that they're also more likely to generate a speedier response.

To be effective, the handwriting must be your own. I've heard of one organisation who employs people to handwrite sales letters for clients. Nope. That's fake.

Telephone calls

The decline in telephone calls is one of the biggest changes I've seen in the business environment. I can work on a client's fee-earning floor and not hear a telephone ring for hours on end. Almost everyone has a mobile phone, but they're rarely used for actually *speaking* to anyone. In 2015, Deloitte surveyed 4,000 adults in the UK and found that 25% of smartphone owners hadn't used their devices to make a call in the past week. Three years earlier, that number was 4%. Paul Lee, Deloitte's head of technology, media, and telecoms research, said: 'It is becoming easier to communicate via messages than to speak.'[54]

Unsolicited calls, impersonal call centres, and automated phone menus have downgraded the telephone experience and discouraged people from using the phone to speak to other people.

---

54   James Titcomb, 'Phone calls a thing of the past as Britons use smartphones for everything but phoning', *The Telegraph*, 6 September 2015.

Like your handwriting, your voice is unique, cannot be faked and is instantly recognisable. Tone and content can be flexed in a one-to-one, making it a totally personal experience for the other person. Your voice has the power to convince, reassure, persuade, warm, and excite applying precisely the right nuances.

I predict that the phone call will make a comeback welcomed by all relationship aficionados.

One in-house lawyer of a FTSE 250 company used only Magic or Silver Circle firms. At a private talk he gave to a group of marketing professionals, he confessed that he thought there was very little to choose between them. However, when giving out new work, he always chose the lawyer who phoned to explain a new development and then demonstrated that they had done their homework by explaining the exact relevance to his business, no matter how complex the situation.

Most people will respond to a phone call or handwritten communication, even if that response doesn't happen immediately.

That being said, I'm not ruling out using a phone for judicious text messaging. Propella is, after all, about making the best of the past, present, and future.

Find your own Power of Personal

Personalisation is about being your authentic self and delivering a unique and relevant experience to your stakeholders. I hope *The Power of Personal* has kick-started your own ideas.

I'm always impressed by what clients come up with to express their true commitment to clients, targets, and other stakeholders once they look at the world from their end of the telescope. Invariably, they are also excited by their ideas because they make them feel... human. Some recent examples:

- To support a client going through a challenging transition, the corporate lawyer who, in his own time, sat in on the client's board meetings, free of charge, even though it meant long-distance travel and no time recording. After twelve months, the lawyer's contribution was so highly valued he was given a formal role and became, in more ways than one, a trusted partner. His generosity of spirit, given for the right reasons, was richly rewarded.

- The private-client lawyer who managed to get through the background noise and sign a celebrity client (a whopping Prize) by finding the common ground: the celebrity's beloved pet dogs. How were those pets covered in the will? Celebrity bagged. How many times do you think that celebrity has shared the story with other celebrities?

- The head of a charity responsible for thanking people, largely in the Silent Generation, who had written this charity into their wills. She stopped sending out standardised thank-you letters and started writing personal ones instead. The number of bequests increased directly as a result.

- The financial adviser who helped out an entrepreneur's parents with an investment query even though the investment was small. When that entrepreneur, a classic Eager Beaver, became wealthy, guess who they went to for investment advice?

- The barrister facing intense competition in a niche sector. In his own time and at his own expense, he partnered with a leading law firm to develop his set's bespoke client-service standards using that firm's own client-service standards as a template. He also spoke at their events and invited his contacts as guests. Commercial closeness in action. Result? More work.

Now it's down to you. What could personalisation look like for your clients, targets, contacts, and people? More importantly, how good could it feel?

Did I say this would be easy? Yes.

Did I say it wouldn't necessarily cost anything? Yes.

Did I say it would work? Yes, most definitely.

Did I say this was clever, smart, and rewarding? Yes.

Did I say it would take up a bit of your time? Yes. But I can promise that, armed with the Propella rationale, tools, and techniques to personalise your communications, you will soon start to enjoy the rewards of your efforts.

Next Steps

As potent as The Power of Personal is the power of possibility, and these two are closely connected.

Writing this book has opened up a world of possibilities for me and I know that, as you read it, the same will happen for you.

If you'd like to keep updated with ideas, stories, sharing from other sectors and developments, there are plenty of options.

LinkedIn fans, please connect with me and follow Propella Global.

If Facebook is your thing, I have my author page: @lizwhitakerauthor

There's more about the business on propella.global. We bring *The Power of Personal* to life with Propella Bootcamps, Accelerators, and Propella in Person. Propella Global clients also enjoy access to our exclusive guide *Making The Impersonal, Personal – Applying Propella across the A to Z of the Marketing Mix,* which looks at how you can apply Propella thinking to all your marketing communications from Advertising and Awards right through to Xmas cards and Gen Z.

You are always welcome to contact me directly on liz.whitaker@propella.global. Feel free to share with me how *The Power of Personal* has worked for you.

I live by the principles in my book and I'd be pleased to hear from you.

Acknowledgements

Writing *The Power of Personal* has been a team effort. A very big team.

I would like to thank the following people for their contribution, many of you with more than one role:

Everyone at Propella HQ – David Hamlett (director of common sense), Marianne Gable (aka LG), Lee Robertson, Kevin Smith, John Elliott, Sarah Gabbitas.

For advising on trademark and IP issues – Lucy Walker and David Harris at Barker Brettell.

My clients and employers who have helped me to test Propella as it evolved – thank you for your ideas and encouragement. Too numerous to mention, but you know who you are: Wragge & Co (now Gowling WLG); Susan Dunn, Stephen O'Dowd and Rocco Pirozzolo at Harbour Litigation Funding; Natasha Harrison and Linda Penfold at Boies Schiller Flexner (UK); Dr Jacomijn van Haersolte-van Hof and Nadine

Amarasinghe at the London Court of International Arbitration; Chris Nott and Elin Pinnell at Capital Law plus Paula Morris now at Darwin Gray; Kate Ive at Pension Partners; Elizabeth Isaacs QC at St Ives Chambers; Lawrie Philpott at Philpott Black; Maeve Jackson previously at Farrer & Co; Jo Thornell previously at SHMA; Clive Mieville and members at Mackrell International; Nick O'Hara at Thursfields; Deborah Baxter at Baxter Harries; John-George Willis at Tughans; Declan Cushley at Pangea Net; Jonathan Davies now at Serjeants' Inn; others at Wesleyan, Family Law in Partnership, Saffery Champness, and Cornwall Street Chambers.

The brilliant team at Ascend Studios for taking my idea and converting it into business intelligence software and creating the brilliant Propella brand. Thank you Jim Walton, Paul Croxton, Stuart Brown, Yarron Frauenfelder, and Craig Edward Passmore (Xanda).

Andy Thornley, Lynne Jones, and Andrew Hopkins at HTDL who created the Propella prototype, Condor Connector.

Those of you who provided me with valuable signposting along the way – Richard Goold, now at E&Y; John Monks at the Pace Partnership; Glyn Morris at Higgs & Sons; Clare Rodway at Kysen PR; Iain Maclean at The Maclean Partnership; Matthew Stafford at 9others; Derek Southall at Hyperscale Group; Pete Gable at Pete Gable Leadership Coaching; Sally Bibb at Engaging Minds; Andy Bounds; Nicola Lynch; Anja Potze; and Fabienne Charles.

Lucy McCarraher, Joe Gregory, and the team at Rethink Press for your can-do attitude and for getting me through the highs and the lows of book publication.

All the people who have contributed so generously to this book with quotes and personal interviews: Susan Dunn, Leslie Gaines-Ross, Nigel Ewington, Larry Hochman, Cathy Walton, Professor Moira Clark, Scott Keyser, Susan Payton, Erik Devaney, Mark Cooper, Rachel Maguire, Sally Mewies, Professor Robin Dunbar, Peter Rees QC, Nicola Duke, Judie Caunce, and David Fennell.

My brilliant, honest, and generous test readers, including Paul Richmond at Grogroup, Grant Anthony and Paul Blythe at Crowe, Simon Slater at Pemberton Greenish, Nicola Mumford, Jenny Hardy at Gowling WLG, Ewan McPhie, Mick Gillick MBE, Kate Hardy, and Kathryn Hobbs.

The sisterhood in the legal community for spurring me on: Toni Pincott, Tamara Littleton, Liz Rivers, Hetty Einzig, Esther Stanhope, Merlie Calvert, Caroline Goodman, Lisa Springate, Lindsay Scott, Brie Stevens-Hoare QC, and Phillipa Charles.

The Book Club sisterhood who kept me nailed to the task!

Daniel Priestley at Dent Global: thank you for writing your books that 'spoke' to me and gave me the formula to build Propella. Huge thanks to the entrepreneur community at Dent Global and especially my accountability group of Carra Santos, Derek Allen Mason, Deon van Niekerk, Alan Davidson, and Katie Young.

My friends and family for keeping me sane but accountable: Sue Moore, the Tylers, Iain and Wendy Elliot, Louise English, Sarah Allcock, Melanie Goddard.

My Mum and Dad: Anne and Cliff Whitaker (my dad sadly passed away in 2016 but read the first book proposal); my stepson, Major Julian Hill; his mother Aurora; Aunt Gemma and wife Briony; my granddaughters Miranda and Clemmie Hill for constantly asking, 'Where's your book, Lizieeeeeee?'

Finally, and most importantly, my wonderful husband Peter Hill who has kept the show on the road.

The Author

 Liz Whitaker is the founder and managing director of Propella Global and creator of Propella, the business intelligence software programme. She has been working with professional services organisations for over 30 years, helping them to use communications to grow their businesses and retain and recruit top talent. Liz advises large, small, international, regional, and boutique firms, as well as membership associations and organisations supplying the professional services sector. Her in-house and consultancy clients have included KPMG, Wragge & Co (now Gowling WLG), Baker McKenzie (graduate recruitment), Harbour Litigation Funding, LCIA, Mackrell International, Grant Thornton, Capital Law, Boies Schiller Flexner (UK), Tughans, Pension Partners, and several barristers' chambers.

Liz holds diplomas from the Chartered Institute of Marketing and the Chartered Institute of Public Relations. Other professional development training includes Ashridge Business School Leadership programme and Directing Strategic Marketing in Professional Firms at Cranfield School of Management.

Liz gives regular presentations and workshops on The Power of Personal to leadership teams, partners and fee earners, and marketing professionals.

Printed in Great Britain
by Amazon